Addiction Essentials

Addiction Essentials

The Go-To Guide for Clinicians and Patients

CARLTON K. ERICKSON

W.W. NORTON & COMPANY

NEW YORK • LONDON

For information about permission to reproduce selections
from this book, write to Permissions, W. W. Norton & Company, Inc.,
500 Fifth Avenue, New York, NY 10110

For information about special discounts for bulk purchases,
please contact W. W. Norton
Special Sales at specialsales@wwnorton.com or 800-233-4830

Manufacturing by R.R. Donnelley, Bloomsburg
Book design by Gilda Hannah
Production manager: Leeann Graham

Library of Congress Cataloging-in-Publication Data

Erickson, Carlton K.
    Addiction essentials: the go-to guide for clinicians and patients /
Carlton K. Erickson.—1st ed.
        p. cm.
Includes bibliographical references and index.
ISBN 978-0-393-70615-4 (pbk.)
1. Substance abuse—Handbooks, manuals, etc. I. Title.
RC564.15.E75 2010
616.86—dc22   2010054020

ISBN: 978-0-393-70615-4 (pbk.)

W. W. Norton & Company, Inc., 500 Fifth Avenue, New York, N.Y. 10110
www.wwnorton.com
W. W. Norton & Company Ltd., Castle House, 75/76 Wells Street,
London W1T 3QT

1 2 3 4 5 6 7 8 9 0

The dedication in my last book to my family can now be expanded, since we have grown. To my giving and beautiful wife, Eunice, and our children, their spouses, and our grandchildren: Steig (Sheri, Emma, Austin, and Jacob); Dirk (Jennifer, Garrett, and Adalyn); Annika Bennett (Bill, Hunter, Luke, and Blaise); and Hans (Mandy, Hayden, and Kennedy)—this book is dedicated to you. (If I write another book in the future, I expect this list will be even longer, as we become even more blessed!)

Contents

Acknowledgments

As a pharmacologist and former mouse researcher, and as a nonrecovering person and an addiction science educator, I am fortunate to have the privilege of interacting with key people within and outside the science community. From the best alcohol and drug researchers, to CEOs and presidents of major treatment centers, to people in recovery around the world, my presentations and writings have been influenced by their shared knowledge, insight, and friendship. I interact almost daily with other research scientists, with my colleagues and friends on the executive council of the Betty Ford Institute, with my colleagues at the Hazelden Foundation, and with my many close friends in recovery. All of this input has helped me to have a unique perspective, as an educator, on the interface among those in the throes of alcohol and other drug addiction, those in recovery from this disease, and those who are studying its causes. Anytime I see a clinician nodding in approval when I mention a new research breakthrough, I know that something magical happens when the science explains the symptoms. For decades, it seems that those who were working on treating people with alcohol and drug problems had no use for research. It was as if they were saying, "we have all the tools to help, and you scientists are just spending money that could better be used for treatment." Today, evidence-based programs are beginning to dominate treatment philosophy and outcomes. Even though 12-step programs still predominate in helping people with "addiction", as they should at this point in history, people now understand that new scientific findings are helping those who cannot or will not be helped by 12-step programs. It is the education of the clinicians and their patients by scientists who are making this happen.

My close friends in recovery every day remind me of the importance of spreading new science to clinicians and students, as well as to the public. John O., Hank M., Mike R., John A., and Kyle E.—you are the inspiration behind my work.

Two colleagues, both of whom are premier educators, have helped make this book a reality. My first graduate student at the University of

Texas at Austin, Mark Evan Goldman, is now a distinguished scientist in his own right living in San Diego. He volunteered to help me write several of the chapters in this book. Mark and I of course think much alike, and he wrote chapters where I was lagging, and even gave me a draft of a chapter that neither he nor I knew much about so that I could finish it. On the other side of the country, my longtime colleague in Albany, Peter Pociluyko, is one of the best clinician-educators I have ever met. Peter had helped me with the clinical vignettes in my last book, so I was aware of his clinical knowledge and accuracy, two characteristics that were critical in writing this book. Peter was able to contribute with those chapters where I was not an expert. Both of these gentlemen insisted not only on helping me write the book, but also on helping me edit it, and to have a final look at the chapters before sending it to the publisher. I will forever be indebted to these two Samaritans who unselfishly added to the excellence of this manuscript.

While many of my colleagues are still searching for book publishers, somehow the people at W.W. Norton saw something in my knowledge and writing that caused them to take a chance on me to write a second book for them. This is to my advantage, since Deborah Malmud is the kind of editor every author would like: supportive, respectful, and knowledgeable. It was her initiative that pointed me in the direction of this book, which is much different from my previous Norton book, *The Science of Addiction: From Neurobiology to Treatment* (2007). This new book is much broader, has a different audience, and was a bigger challenge to write because of its breadth and depth in several areas of addiction in which I was not trained. Thank you, Deborah.

CARLTON K. ERICKSON, PhD
Austin, Texas

Addiction Essentials

CHAPTER 1

Causes of Addiction

PATIENTS' OVERVIEW

The patient should understand that research in the areas of neurobiology and genetics has now reached a point where we know many of the causes of the disease of chemical dependence. This is not the same as "drug abuse." The disease of chemical dependence has a very large genetic component, which—when combined with prolonged use of a drug—leads to neuroadaptation of the brain's reward or pleasure pathway (the mesolimbic dopamine system [MDS]). Neuroadaptation is the cause of the pathway's dysregulation, leading to abnormal messages being sent to the frontal lobes. Thus the frontal lobes fail to act to control drug use, and the person suffers from an inability to control impulses associated with drug use. This is the brain disease of chemical dependence, loosely called "addiction."

When discussing the causes of "addiction," it is first important to understand what "addiction" is and what it is not. *Addiction* is a term that is widely misunderstood by most people. When a U.S. president states that "our nation is addicted to oil," most people understand that the United States has a fixation on oil or that the nation is heavily dependent on oil as a source of energy. Heroin "addiction" is known by most people to be a case where heroin users develop a habit of using heroin or just that people use heroin, an illegal drug. People with a "tanning-booth addiction" are thought to use tanning booths so much that their risk for skin cancer increases. "BlackBerry addiction" has recently prompted people to refer to the device as a

"CrackBerry." Finally, we know, because of newspaper and magazine articles, that the following have been called "addictions": love of rugs, love of lingerie, love of certain flavors of ice cream or candy, love of exercise, love of food, love of computers, love of pornography, love of videogames, to name a few.

To an addiction scientist, the word *addiction* most appropriately describes obsessive thinking and compulsion for legal or illegal drugs used in the face of adverse consequences. Whereas there is a lot of scientific evidence for drug addictions, there is not yet a consensus on whether behaviors are addicting. Thus the best diagnostic manuals for psychiatric disorders do not use the term *addiction*. The large number of definitions in popular use (search the term on Google) illustrates the great misunderstandings that people have about "addiction."

The problem with the word *addiction* is that it is the basis of so many myths. Here are a few:

- Caffeine is addicting.
- Marijuana is not addicting.
- Nasal decongestants are addicting.
- Crack babies are born addicted.
- Pregnant women taking methadone have babies born addicted to methadone.
- Antidepressants are addicting.
- Physicians must restrict opiate painkiller medication doses for fear of addiction.
- Obese people are addicted to food.
- Addiction is a habit.
- The greater the euphoria (high) produced by a drug, the more addicting it is.
- The more a drug is available, the more addicting it is.
- The more information children have about drugs, the more likely they are to become addicted.

Have you heard of these? They are all scientifically incorrect, unless you want to use your own definition of *addiction*.

Most scientists these days are recognizing that *addiction* is an imprecise term and that other terms can help people better understand the causes and treatment of this disease. The more appropriate term, *dependence*, will be discussed fully in Chapter 2, "Diagnosis of Drug Overuse and Mental Disorders." In brief, what we call chemical dependence is a brain disease that can be diagnosed, just as psychiatrists diagnose different types of clinical depression, anxiety, or, for example, attention deficit/hyperactivity disorder (ADHD). Chemical dependence is a different drug-overuse condition than is *drug abuse,* a term that describes a voluntary drug-overuse situation in which people use bad judgment in drinking too much alcohol or using an illegal drug such as cocaine or crack. Drug abuse is the cause of many socioeconomic problems in the nation, but it is not a brain disease. For the most part, this book will be talking about chemical dependence (also known as drug addiction): its causes, impacts on individuals and the family, and its treatment. (Chemical dependence is not the same as physiological or physical dependence; the latter is related to the adaptation of body systems to a drug to the point where withdrawal signs and symptoms appear when drug use is stopped.)

Chemical dependence ("dependence") is a recognized diagnostic entity in the *Diagnostic and Statistical Manual of Mental Disorders, Fourth Edition, Text Revision (DSM-IV-TR [2000]),* published by the American Psychiatric Association. It is diagnosed when an individual exhibits three or more characteristics (criteria, out of seven total) listed in the *DSM-IV-TR* monograph (see Chapter 2 of this book). Once an individual is diagnosed with this disease, the next question is how that person can be treated. In general, the more severe the disease (somewhat indicated by the number of criteria met by the person), the more difficult it is to treat. However, there are many factors (e.g., lifestyle, supportive individuals in a person's life, financial resources, level of education, resilience) that determine a person's outcome (i.e., recovery) when going through treatment. These factors will be covered in later chapters.

(Note: At this writing, the *DSM* Committee on Substance-Related Disorders is considering a new monograph for the fifth edition of *DSM,* to be published in 2013. The committee has recommended that the terms *abuse* and *dependence* be replaced with the term *substance use disorders* and placed in a new section of *DSM-V* called "Addiction and Related Disorders." If this recommendation remains in the final edition, much of the terminology discussed above will revert back to the older and less scientifically precise term, *addiction.*)

Operating Assumptions of Addiction Theories

Addiction is typically viewed in one of several ways and each perspective involves several assumptions. A classic psychiatric model argues that addiction is symptomatic of an unresolved conflict or past trauma or is a method to self-medicate psychiatric symptoms. A biological toxic-induced disease model argues that individuals are genetically predisposed and that they were "addicts waiting to happen" and just need the last ingredient of a drug to trigger symptoms of the disease. Another model is that addiction is due to moral or character defects and that use of any intoxicant or psychoactive drug is immoral, so addiction is the result of immoral behavior. A view common to Alcoholics Anonymous (AA) and Narcotics Anonymous is that addiction is a disease affecting the body, mind, and spirit; it requires abstinence to get better. Classic learning theory proclaims that addiction is a learned and conditioned behavior, resulting from positive and then negative reinforcement; it might also propose that addiction is due to poor social and coping skills that evolve into "adaptive behaviors." Some family systems theories view addiction as symptomatic of family anxiety and dysfunctional interactions between the individual and family; the addicted person may also be seen as "holding others hostage" and that the family is a "victim." A more contemporary family systems view sees addictive behavior as a biological illness that causes difficulties for the individual and family.

It is no wonder, then, that the public and policy makers are confused about addiction and that scientists with different training and backgrounds disagree about the causes of addiction. Today, contemporary addiction practitioners and scientists view chemical dependence ("addiction") according to a neurobiological disease model with strong influence of genetic risk factors. In addition, many scientists and practitioners also recognize that environmental and psychosocial factors play a significant role in onset and progression of the disease. With this in mind, drugs can activate, deactivate, or trigger gene expression, and psychoactive drugs can also rewire neurobiological connections. This in turn affects conscious and unconscious behavior, thinking, and emotions. Yet we also know that behavior, thinking, and environmental factors (such as stress and fear) can influence gene expression and change neurobiology. In other words, "neurochemistry affects psychology" and "psychology affects neurochemistry." In terms of the spirituality of recovery so commonly discussed at AA meetings, one AA person has said that he believes that "God works through molecules, most of the time."

Biological Factors

Addiction has been called a biopsychosocial genetic disease, indicating there are many factors that contribute to its cause. In fact, the latest neurobiological/genetic research indicates its origins are primarily biological, with genetics playing a major role in its causation, leading to major psychological and social problems in the affected individual. In other words, what were formerly thought to be psychological causes (e.g., weak will, unresolved unconscious conflict) or social causes (e.g., poor socioeconomic environment) of addiction are now seen either as contributors to initial use and early continued drug use (supporting the development of chemical dependence in vulnerable individuals) or as sequelae (effects) of the disease. For example, clinical depression often accompanies the use of many drugs over a long period and can be a precursor to the long-term use of drugs. Clinical depression can also follow prolonged drug use. The social effects of chemical dependence include stigma, prejudice, disrupted families, reduced job performance, and the giving up of important social activities in order to seek and use drugs.

Nondrug Addictions

Nondrug addictions have been called behavioral addictions, process addictions, and activity addictions. These inappropriately (according to *DSM-IV-TR*) include gambling, Internet, video-gaming, exercise, food, and pornography. Unfortunately the media and general public use the word *addiction* in its broadest, nonscientific sense: addiction to oil, tanning-booth addiction, cell-phone addiction, even lingerie addiction.

In the current edition of *DSM-IV-TR*, the word *addiction* is not used. The only nondrug "addiction" mentioned is gambling, and it is described as "compulsive gambling disorder," found in the section on "impulse control disorders not otherwise classified." Early recommendations for the *DSM-V* are that the new edition will feature a section on addiction and related disorders, and will include gambling. "Internet addiction" will be included in the Appendix, until further research validates that it has similar brain mechanisms as gambling or drug addiction (these recommendations might change before publication in 2013).

About 99% of the research on addictions has been carried out on drugs (chemicals). Thus, to include other behavioral conditions in the *DSM* will take a great deal of research. How much research is enough to change the classification of other nondrug addictions? This will be answered by the composition and attitudes of future *DSM* committees. In the meantime, it is best not to use the word *addiction* to describe the compulsive behaviors listed above.

Is "Addiction" a Choice?

This idea of choice as a cause of addiction has been popular for centuries, and no one has ever come to a conclusion, until now. When the drug overuse conditions of drug abuse and chemical dependence are studied, it is clear that making a choice to use the drug is a major factor in drug abuse, but not in chemical dependence. Drug abusers make poor or sound (i.e., "bad" or "good") decisions or choices about drug use. They make choices because they have control over whether they use the drug or not, and to use in excess or only in moderation. People who have developed chemical dependence, on the other hand, no longer have a choice over whether to use the drug. This is because the brain chemistry has changed so that the frontal lobes (where choice-making occurs) are no longer functioning normally. The cause of the frontal lobe malfunction is a dysregulation (something that has gone wrong) in the brain's reward pathway. This, then, is the disease of chemical dependence. The person no longer has a choice to use a drug any more than a person with schizophrenia can stop hearing voices. "But they shouldn't have used the drug in the first place" is what the "choice proponents" shout! This makes no sense, because no drug causes 100% of people to develop dependence, and no one will refrain from using a drug for fear of addiction (dependence). Also, what about those 5-year-old children on the school ground who take a drug because a pusher offers it to them? Do these children have the knowledge or life skills to say no?

People are so afraid that calling this a disease will somehow give people an excuse to use drugs. Does calling a cancer a carcinoma give people an excuse to lie out in the sun? This is nonsense. Another fear is that diseased addicts will no longer be held responsible for their drinking and drugging. But people will always be held responsible for their behavior (even if drug-induced), so this is also an unreasonable concern.

To summarize, if we wish to use the sloppy term *addiction*, then there is a choice involved in taking the drug, because *addiction* means "I really like it and don't want to stop." Using the proper scientific and clinical terminology of *abuse* and *dependence*, then choice is involved in the cause of drug abuse, but not in the cause of the brain disease of chemical dependence. (Sadly, it appears the terms *abuse* and *dependence* may be on the way out in *DSM-V*.)

The Contribution of Genetics

Genetics plays a large role in the production of chemical dependence, because up to 60% of the causes of alcohol dependence appear to be due to genetic vulnerability. (We know less about the genetic incidence of other chemical dependence, but it also appears to be high for such chemical dependence as cocaine dependence, heroin dependence, and nicotine dependence.) Not everyone who overuses drugs "has what it takes" to develop chemical dependence. This is seen in Table 1.1 below, which lists the lifetime risk for developing dependence associated with the various groups of drugs. Factors involved with "having what it takes" to develop the disease involve genetics and as yet unidentified psychological, environmental, and other lifestyle factors.

In the case of nicotine, Table 1.1 illustrates that the use of this drug leads to dependence in 32% of the users. In the case of heroin, only 23% of the users will ever become dependent ("addicted"); the rest of the us-

TABLE 1.1	
Estimated Lifetime Risk for Developing Dependence	
Drug	**% Risk**
Nicotine	32
Heroin	23
Cocaine powder	17
Crack cocaine	20
Alcohol	15
Amphetamines	11
Cannabis	9
"Sedatives" (benzodiazepines)	9
Analgesic opioids (e.g., methadone)	9
Psychedelics (e.g., LSD)	5
Inhalants	4

Adapted from Anthony et al. (1994).

ers would be called social users, abusers, misusers, recreational users, or criminals, and they would never become dependent, even if they were to use heroin for their entire lives. This goes against the statement that "all heroin users are addicts." In the case of alcohol, the common statement "If you just drink alcohol long enough, often enough, in high enough amounts, you'll eventually become an alcoholic" just isn't true; it appears that some people are not susceptible to developing the disease of alcohol dependence. In other words, they "don't have what it takes"! It's that way with Parkinson's disease, Type I diabetes, and even hypertension—not everyone is susceptible to developing the disease. So it appears that, as with other diseases, chemical dependence shares the characteristic of individual susceptibility.

We know that chemical dependence runs in families. We know that if one identical sibling (in twins, triplets, or other multiple births) develops chemical dependence, the chances are significantly higher that the other identical sibling(s) will develop the disease, even if they are reared apart their entire lives. We know that adoptees have a high rate of chemical dependence, even if they are adopted out into non-chemically dependent families. We know that chemical dependence is a polygenetic disease, meaning that there are multiple genes involved in the vulnerability to the disease. Finally, we know that genes are not destiny. Dependence can appear to skip generations, and everyone in a chemically dependent family does not have an equal risk for developing the disease. Behavioral, environmental, and social factors can also influence gene expression and may help impede or support the onset of the disease.

It is even more important to realize that the brain-related causes—which are called dysregulation—are driven by genes. The causes of dysregulation appear to be related to gene alleles (gene variants) that cause abnormal protein formation in the nerves.

The MDS

The MDS, also known as the medial forebrain bundle, the pleasure pathway, or the reward pathway (all synonyms), is where chemical dependence occurs in the brain. The MDS can easily be identified by placing two fingers (in the form of a V) on the forehead and another finger above either ear, and then imagining where the lines between the fingers cross in the middle of the brain. This pathway, running from the center of the brain to the frontal lobes, encompasses other specific areas: the amygdala, the nucleus accumbens, and the ventral tegmental area.

When a drug activates the MDS, the person experiences a feeling of pleasure (also called euphoria, a feeling of being "high"). When a susceptible individual uses a drug over a long period of time, the pathway might be altered in its function (and perhaps microanatomy) to become dysregulated. This neuroadaptive change is at the core of the cause of chemical dependence, for now the pathway is sending erroneous messages to the frontal lobes, causing them to malfunction. The normal function of the frontal lobes is an "executive" one, meaning that it normally operates to allow proper decision-making, judgment calls, and control of impulses. Thus, abnormal function means that the person now operates on impulse, has poor judgment, and makes poor decisions. This is at the heart of the "impaired control over drug use" that characterizes chemical dependence. The brain is now saying, "I can't stop using drugs without help." Thus "willpower" and "choice" are taken out of the equation (and conscious control over drug use is lost), for the person's brain is now saying, to the drug, "You're what I've been waiting for all my life, and I'm not going to let you go." And the drinking or drugging continues until the person dies or until treatment is initiated.

The Stages of "Addiction"

According to some experts (Koob & Volkow, 2010), drug addiction is a disorder that involves elements of impulsivity, obsessive thinking, and compulsivity leading to an addiction cycle with three stages. These stages are (a) initial use/binge/intoxication, (b) withdrawal/negative affect, and (c) preoccupation/anticipation (craving). There appear to be discrete brain circuits involved with each stage: (Stage 1) ventral tegmental area and ventral striatum, (Stage 2) extended amygdala, and (Stage 3) orbitofrontal cortex–dorsal striatum, prefrontal cortex, basolateral amygdala, hippocampus, and insula (craving) and the cingulate gyrus, dorsolateral prefrontal, and inferior frontal cortices (disrupted inhibitory control). The transition to addiction (Stage 3) involves neuroadaptation in all of the above structures, beginning with changes in the MDS and then involving all the other structures. (For the non-neuroanatomist, these structures have been discovered through animal and human imaging research to be involved in these functions. They are all neurally interconnected with, and through, the MDS, which is central to the development of addiction.)

Environmental and Psychological Causes

Geneticists talk about the environment affecting genetic influence in the cause of diseases, so certainly the environment is involved as one of the causes of chemical dependence. The problem is that we don't know which characteristics of the environment are involved, to what extent, or how the environment affects a person's vulnerability to dependence. Unlike with drug abuse (conscious decision to use in excess), where the environment plays a huge causative role, environment or psychological stress alone does not directly cause chemical dependence. For example, it is difficult to imagine that a "poor socioeconomic neighborhood" could powerfully and specifically produce dysregulation of the MDS. On the other hand, posttraumatic stress disorder (PTSD) would certainly be powerful enough to change brain function, but can it specifically dysregulate the MDS to cause an increased incidence of chemical dependence? Or is the effect of PTSD to create greater drug-use risks that make the person more susceptible to developing a drug use disorder? Can physical trauma of the brain dysregulate the MDS? How about childhood wounding (physical abuse, emotional abuse, or sexual abuse)? How about an emotional divorce affecting a spouse or children? Until research shows otherwise, many scientists believe that such emotional and environmental factors are most likely to increase drug use and abuse, which could trigger chemical dependence in those who "have what it takes" (i.e., those individuals who are vulnerable to the disease).

In a classic case of scientific detective work (Langston & Irwin, 1986), a neurologist observed several instances of Parkinson's disease–like symptoms in drug abusers and eventually identified the culprit as a neu-rotoxin (MPTP [1-methyl-4-phenyl-1,2,3,6-tetrahydropyridine]) from a failed attempt at synthesis of an opiate. Although the abuser's goal was to make a "synthetic heroin," injection of the resulting toxin caused a rapid onset of Parkinson's disease–like symptoms that were reduced with stan-dard anti–Parkinson's disease therapies. Following continued abuse, the first patient died from a drug overdose, allowing the opportunity for an autopsy to be performed. The autopsy revealed destruction of a specific brain area (substantia nigra), typically seen in elderly Parkinson's dis-ease patients. These events led to a new understanding of the causes of Parkinson's disease.

Unfortunately, we have no such historical story of accidental discov-ery of the causes of chemical dependence. More than likely, the details of the dysregulation of the mesolimbic dopamine pathway will prove to be much more subtle, and more elusive, than the relatively large changes in the brain that are related to Parkinson's disease. However, it is clear that subtle changes in the brain (in this case, the MDS) can lead to ma-jor behavioral changes of a long-lasting nature—as in not being able to control the consumption of alcohol, nicotine, and other drugs. We await the discovery of those exact changes, which will undoubtedly be found through future research.

CHAPTER 2

Diagnosis of Drug Overdose and Mental Disorders

with Peter J. Pociluyko, MA, CASAC, CCS

PATIENTS' OVERVIEW

After discussing the causes of addiction, it is time to look at current diagnostic categories in order to set the stage for later discussions. It is also important for the patient to understand that psychiatrists and other clinicians are now able to diagnose mental disorders with the help of established diagnostic manuals. Accurate diagnosis and understanding of the individual's disorder are critical for proper treatment. This chapter discusses most important psychiatric disorder categories related to drug overuse. The presence of a mental disorder and a drug use disorder together make treatment of either or both more difficult, and it is important to find a clinician who understands these diagnostic categories.

A simple overarching definition of mental illness, also called mental disease, or mental disorder, is: "Any of various psychiatric conditions, usually characterized by impairment of an individual's normal cognitive, emotional, or behavioral functioning, and caused by physiological or psychosocial factors" (American Heritage Medical Dictionary, 2007). By this definition, addiction is a mental illness, although in practice addiction and mental disorder are considered to be separate, perhaps because people with drug addiction don't like to be thought of as "mentally ill." However, there are many ways in which they are alike: People with "addiction" are known to have "impaired control" over their use of drugs, and those who are mentally ill have "impaired control" over their senses and thoughts (schizophrenia), their mood and behavior (depression and bipolar disorder), or their course of illness (continues unless treated). In both addiction and mental disorders, there is a genetic component in the causation, and the environment initiates or exacerbates the condition. Indeed, addiction and mental disorders both run in families.

The comorbidity connection between addiction and other mental disorders is well known. Also called dual diagnosis, addiction is comorbid with depression, bipolar disorder, anxiety, panic, attention-deficit hyperactivity disorders (ADHD), posttraumatic stress disorder (PTSD), schizophrenia, and other Axis I and Axis II disorders. Researchers have estimated that 37% of adults with an alcohol-related disorder have another mental disorder at some time in their lives. Even more (53%) with a history of *other* drug abuse or dependence have experienced a mental disorder (National Alliance on Mental Illness, 2010). Mental health problems often predate drug use problems by 4–6 years. Thus, alcohol or other drugs may be a form of self-medication to alleviate the mental disorder symptoms. In some cases, drug use disorder precedes the development of mental health problems. For example, anxiety and depression may occur as a response to stressors from broken relationships or lost employment related to a drug-using lifestyle.

Nearly 50% of persons with schizophrenia have a drug use disorder (National Alliance on Mental Illness, 2010). Among those with bipolar disorder, 61% have a drug use disorder, which most commonly appears during a manic phase. Overall, a patient with anxiety disorder has about a 33% chance of abusing or being dependent on drugs or alcohol. With regard to PTSD, 52% abuse alcohol or are dependent on it, and 35% have other drug abuse or dependence issues (Tull, 2010). The smoking rate among PTSD patients is about double that of the general population, and the rate of other drug abuse and dependence is almost 3 times that of the general population.

With respect to drug use in the homeless, two thirds of homeless people report that drugs (including alcohol) were a major reason for their becoming homeless. It has been estimated that about 38% of homeless people are dependent on alcohol, with 26% of the homeless abusing other drugs. While drug abuse is most common in homeless youth and young adults, alcohol abuse is more common in the elderly homeless (National Coalition for the Homeless, 2009).

Substance (Drug, Chemical) Abuse

Drug abuse is a drug overuse condition described in the *DSM-IV-TR (2000)* as a maladaptive pattern of drug use leading to impairment or distress, presenting as one or more of four diagnostic characteristics in a 12-month period. These characteristics are (a) recurrent drug use leading to failure to fulfill major (family, occupational, social) obligations, (b) recurrent drug use that is physically hazardous, (c) recurrent drug-related legal problems, and (d) continued drug use despite social or interpersonal problems. Most descriptions of drug abuse indicate that this drug overuse problem is volitional, preventable, and not a disease. Thus people who use drugs recreationally or to get high or to be sociable can and often do abuse drugs, and there is a terrible toll in terms of costs to society and on families, as well as on the drug abusers themselves. (Note: *Drug abuse* is often a catchall term for all drug overuse conditions, and most of the public and policy makers thus see all drug overuse as a nuisance, often criminal, activity where irresponsible people are using drugs too much, too often. However, as seen below in the "Chemical Dependence" section, a segment of drug overuse is a medical problem—the disease of "addiction.")

Substance (Drug, Chemical) Dependence

Drug abuse as described above is not the same as chemical dependence. Chemical dependence is another drug overuse condition, described in the *DSM-IV-TR (2000)* as a maladaptive pattern of drug use, leading to impairment or distress, presenting as three or more of seven diagnostic characteristics in a 12-month period. These characteristics are (a) tolerance to the drug's actions, (b) withdrawal signs and symptoms upon cessation of use of the drug, (c) the drug is used more frequently or in greater quantity than intended, (d) there is an inability to control drug use, (e) effort is expended to obtain the drug, (f) important activities are replaced by drug use, and (g) drug use continues despite knowledge of a persistent physical or psychological problem. Most descriptions of chemical dependence (popularly known as "addiction") indicate that this drug overuse problem is not volitional, not preventable when a person is using a drug, and is a disease. In the case of chemical dependence, drug use is not under the control of the individual. The diagnostic characteristics listed above indicate that the person has "impaired control over the use of a drug," and the impaired control is now known to be caused by a problem with the brain's reward pathway (scientifically, the mesolimbic dopamine system [MDS], as discussed in Chapter 1). Authors who argue against the "disease concept of addiction" usually do not know or understand the complete neurobiological and genetic scientific findings that have been accumulating over the past several decades—findings that clearly indicate that a dysregulation of the brain's reward pathway (involving the brain's frontal lobes, which regulate impulses, decision making, and judgment) causes an inability of the diseased person to consciously control his or her use of drugs.

DSM-IV

The *Diagnostic and Statistical Manual of Mental Disorders, Fourth Edition (DSM-IV)*, and its Text Revision (*DSM-IV-TR*) are diagnostic manuals published by the American Psychiatric Association in 1994 and 2000, respectively. The manual is a diagnostic guide for physicians and others who want to provide accurate diagnoses for psychiatric disorders, including drug abuse, chemical dependence, and the mental disorders listed below. (A similar diagnostic manual, the *ICD-10 Classification of Mental and Behavioural Disorders: Clinical Descriptions and Diagnostic Guidelines [1992]*, is published by the World Health Organization.) Whereas disorders such as diabetes and hypertension can be diagnosed by objective measures (blood glucose and blood pressure, respectively), psychiatric illnesses must be diagnosed currently through more subjective, weight-of-the-evidence measures, such as those listed above for drug abuse and chemical dependence. Thus the tools used to diagnose psychiatric disorders can change with emerging research and clinical findings. The next editions of *DSM* and *ICD*, due to be published around 2013, are likely to be different from the current editions, because evidence about the characteristics of diseases often changes. One anticipated change is the insertion of a section titled "Addiction and Related Disorders," under which a category of "Substance Use Disorders" will replace current sections on substance abuse and substance dependence. In addition, most major psychiatric category diagnostic criteria will be updated and in some cases overhauled to reflect the research that has accumulated over the past two decades. Thus the descriptors of the following mental disorders will be kept general in the descriptions below, in case there are major changes in the upcoming *DSM-V*.

The *DSM-IV-TR (2000)* states that the appropriate use of its contents requires extensive clinical training and that laypersons should consult the *DSM* only to obtain information, not to make diagnoses. Furthermore, people who may have a mental disorder should be advised to consult a professional for treatment, because the *DSM* does not contain recommendations for treatment. Untrained individuals should certainly not use the *DSM* to diagnose themselves or others because of possible emotional bias. The professional is trained to understand comorbid (co-occurring) disorders, family issues, and medications that the patient is taking or should be taking.

The *DSM-IV-TR (2000)* uses a "multi-axial system" for categorization of mental disorders. This consists of five levels of psychiatric diagnosis according to different aspects of disorder or disability. The first two levels are of most importance as being comorbid with drug use disorders:

Axis I mental disorders are clinical disorders, including major mental disorders, drug use disorders, and developmental and learning disorders as listed and described in the *DSM-IV-TR (2000)*. The common mental disorders that clinicians may encounter are bipolar disorder, schizophrenia, anxiety disorders, PTSD, major depression, and low-grade depression (sometimes called dysthymic disorder). These conditions are often accompanied by one or more drug use disorders, such as abuse or dependence on alcohol, nicotine, opioids, sedative hypnotics, stimulants, or cannabis. However, many acute psychiatric symptoms are indistinguishable from symptoms of drug use or withdrawal, and symptoms of drug use and withdrawal can be indistinguishable from psychiatric illness.

Axis II disorders include personality disorders, maladaptive personality traits, and significant ego-defenses. Patients often have additional Axis II personality disorders, most commonly borderline personality disorder (BPD), antisocial personality disorder (APD or ASPD; APD will be used throughout this book), narcissistic personality disorder (NPD), paranoid personality disorder, or histrionic personality disorder (HPD) (in which a person acts emotional or dramatic in order to get attention), and obsessive-compulsive personality disorder (OCD). Some may have mental retardation, a condition that is also listed in this category. People with Axis II disorders are not psychotic, but have rigid, maladaptive personality qualities (traits) that affect their perception, interpretation, reactions, and general behavior, and which result in significant interpersonal, employment, and legal problems. The Axis II scale also allows practitioners to list any significant psychological defenses (ego-defenses) and psychological traits that impair recovery or functioning. While Axis I drug use disorder and mental disorder may initially present as the most pressing concerns for treatment, the failure to address personality disorders will tend to result in poor treatment and recovery outcomes.

Axis III, IV, and V disorders include acute medical conditions and physical factors that do not seem to be comorbid with drug use disorders.

Details of Co-occurring Disorders

Individuals with co-occurring disorders have drug abuse or chemical dependence and a mental disorder at the same time. They may also have more than one drug use and mental disorder at the same time, along with complicating conditions such as a personality disorder, a developmental or learning disability, or other health conditions, such as high blood pressure or cardiac arrhythmias. In the past, common terms (now considered inadequate) were *dual diagnosis, dual disorders, mentally ill and chemically addicted* (**MICA**), and *mentally ill substance user* (**MISA**).

The term *comorbidity* has been used interchangeably with co-occurring disorders; however, this definition has been expanded by some clinicians. Morbidity refers to disease or illness; however, comorbidity can also describe the presence of two or more disorders that interact and affect the course or prognosis of each illness. Within this frame, comorbidity occurs when one condition causes, supports, or negatively affects the course of another. For example, people with frequent bouts of generalized anxiety may consume alcohol regularly to curb their anxious feelings. Gradually they begin binge drinking (more than three standard drinks per day or five per occasion) and do not use more therapeutic methods to control their anxiety. Over time, they develop tolerance, begin to have trouble restricting or limiting their use, and start using in a compulsive manner. They then feel increased anxiety when the alcohol wears off and they drink more, suggesting alcohol dependence and a compounding effect on their anxiety disorder. (It is important for clinicians to know this because medication treatment may differ if a patient has comorbid disorders.)

People use ego-defense mechanisms (psychological defenses) to focus, deflect, postpone, and redirect information, feelings, memories, and ideas. For example, without the ability to temporarily use denial and selective inattention, people would not be able to concentrate and would be continually distracted by too much incoming information. Ego-defenses also reduce the awareness of information that could cause psychological disorientation or disintegration.

The development of rigid ego-defenses is nearly a universal symptom of drug abuse and is equally common for people with a major mental disorder and a personality disorder (in whom it is especially common). An inability to develop effective coping skills prevents people from recognizing and changing behavior. For example, patients can have various forms of denial and minimizing, such as denial of the facts, denial by omission, denial of personal responsibility, denial of their own awareness, or denial of adverse effects of their behavior. Patients with co-occurring disorders tend to use multiple forms of denial and minimizing. An example is denying that one has a drug use disorder or a mental disorder, and denying the negative effects caused by these conditions. It may be that a defense like denial is a patient's last-ditch attempt to maintain dignity and self-worth. People with a co-occurring disorder may also use multiple rationalizations: *I use narcotics because I have a mental disorder. I have a mental disorder due to my drug use. Things are really OK; it is other people who are the problem.*

Narcissism (egotism, vanity) is also a psychological trait common among people with drug abuse and who have personality disorders (this trait is also common in people with pathological gambling, mania, delusional thinking, and paranoid ideation). Along with the use of defenses, narcissism prompts individuals to insist the rules do not apply to them, so they try to defy reality and defy the consequences of their behavior. Narcissism is usually assumed to mean the "love of self"; however, it actually means "love the self-image"—the image a person has constructed. This love of self-image is due to an inability to distinguish between the ideal self (imagined) and the real self (reality), and this conflicting view creates internal feelings of anxiety and psychological tension, often externalized in the form of problem behavior.

Depression

According to TimesWellness.com, depression "is a mental disorder characterized by sustained depression of mood, anhedonia (inability to experience pleasure), sleep and appetite disturbances, and feelings of worthlessness, guilt, and hopelessness." Diagnostic criteria for a major depressive episode (*DSM-IV-TR, 2000*) include a depressed mood, a marked reduction of interest or pleasure in virtually all activities, or both, lasting for at least 2 weeks. In addition, three or more of the following must be present: gain or loss of weight, increased or decreased sleep, increased or decreased level of psychomotor activity, fatigue, feelings of guilt or worthlessness, diminished ability to concentrate, and recurring thoughts of death or suicide. A major depressive disorder is a *DSM* diagnosis that is established when the specified criteria are met. Depression is often observed when alcohol is overused, when amphetamine or cocaine use is discontinued, and in association with the disease of alcohol dependence.

Bipolar and Cyclothymic Disorder

Bipolar disorder, which was once referred to as manic-depressive disorder, is characterized by cyclical moods that alternate from a period of mania to a period of major depression, then cycles back to a manic episode. Often, periods of normal mood or within-normal-range mood can last for many months or more than a year. However, some patients will have a mood cycle that is very rapid, and they will have four or more cycles of depression and mania within a year. Cyclothymic disorder is similar, but the periods of mania are not as severe or as common and are referred to as hypomania. Some patients may demonstrate a mixed state of manic and depressed symptoms or will appear depressed for a few days, then rapidly cycle to symptoms of mania or milder hypomania for several days before appearing depressed again. Mania, hypomania, and a mixed pattern are often misconstrued as due to stimulant or cannabis use and make it difficult to correctly diagnose a bipolar disorder. Patients will have a "rapid cycle between mania and depression" and have the poorest prognosis for stabilization and reduced recovery risk from drug abuse. They often switch from one type of drug to another depending upon their mood cycle. Alcohol and sedative drugs can partly or completely mask the symptoms of bipolar disorder. Many patients with psychiatric disorders, including those with bipolar disorder, do not want to be labeled as mentally ill or addicted. Often they proclaim, "I am not nuts, and I am not an addict." This dual denial and minimization, which is also seen in people with other Axis I disorders, can make these patients especially difficult to treat. For example, some hypomanic individuals perform better and do not want to be treated to reduce their creativity or to meet obligations such as tight deadlines or expectations. Many people including business leaders and scientists have hypomanic personalities.

Anxiety Disorders

According to the *DSM-IV-TR (2000)*, anxiety disorders are often debilitating chronic conditions. They can either begin suddenly after a triggering event (such as riding in a small airplane) or may be present from an early age (such as fear of thunderstorms). High stress often causes anxiety to flare up, and symptoms include headache, sweating, muscle spasms, palpitations, and high blood pressure leading to fatigue or even exhaustion. The terms *anxiety* and *fear* are often used interchangeably, but clinically these are different conditions. *Anxiety* is defined as an unpleasant emotional state in which the cause is not known or is unavoidable (perhaps due to internal conflict), while *fear* is an emotional and physiological response to a known external threat (such as a tornado). The term *anxiety disorder* includes fears and anxieties; phobias (persistent or irrational fears) make up the majority of anxiety disorder cases. Finally, anxiety disorders often co-occur with clinical depression (about 60% comorbidity). Anxiety disorders often lead to alcohol or benzodiazepine abuse, and can be observed during withdrawal from these drugs.

Obsessive compulsive disorder (OCD) is an anxiety disorder characterized by complaints of persistent or repetitive thoughts (obsessions) or behaviors (compulsions). "Obsessions" are thinking of something all the time, "compulsions" are doing something all the time. Some experts differentiate OCD from "addictive" behaviors by stating that with OCD, the person feels compelled to repeat behaviors in spite of a feeling that the thoughts or behaviors are excessive or inappropriate, and feels distress if they stop them. "Addictive" behaviors, on the other hand, are said to "produce pleasure or gratification." This is out-of-date thinking, illustrating an incomplete understanding of what "addiction" (now called dependence) does to people and how they feel when they cannot stop using drugs. Some experts now believe that addictions are nothing more than a sophisticated form of OCD.

Schizophrenia

According to PsychologyToday.com, schizophrenia is a "disabling, chronic, and severe mental illness in which reality is perceived or expressed abnormally." There may be distortions in perception involving all five senses (sight, hearing, taste, smell, and touch). Most commonly, there are auditory hallucinations, paranoid or bizarre delusions, or disorganized thinking or speech. Patients might also show inappropriate responses to situations. Schizophrenia is often accompanied by the use of drugs such as nicotine and alcohol to reduce symptoms of the disease.

PTSD

Posttraumatic stress disorder (PTSD) is an anxiety disorder, sometimes severe, that can occur in some people after a terrifying event or ordeal in which there was a threat or an occurrence of grave physical harm. It can develop at any age, but these days PTSD is most associated with the violence of combat. However, PTSD is not limited to wartime incidents; it can also result from trauma associated with people witnessing accidents, being victims of violent personal attacks, or being exposed to natural or human-caused disasters. Clinicians understand that there is a strong association between PTSD and drug abuse. Thus PTSD is a risk factor for drug abuse, and among patients with drug use disorders, 30%–60% meet the criteria for co-occurring PTSD. While many clinicians believe that chemical dependence can be induced by PTSD, this has not yet been proven.

BPD

According to *DSM-IV-TR (2000)*, borderline personality disorder (BPD) is a "pervasive pattern of instability of interpersonal relationships, self-image, and affects, and marked impulsivity that begins by early adult-hood and is present in a variety of contexts" (p. 706). Generally there is unusual instability in mood, black-and-white thinking, unstable inter-personal relationships, and a problem with self-image. More often diag-nosed in women, BPD can include other symptoms such as periods of severe depression, anxiety, or irritability; uncontrolled anger; recurring threats of suicide; and uncontrolled characteristics such as overspend-ing, increased sexual activity, drug abuse, reckless driving, shoplifting, binge eating, or self-injurious behavior. BPD may be a risk factor for alcoholism, perhaps because of the association between BPD and drug use to control symptoms of the disorder.

APD

The *DSM-IV-TR (2000)* defines antisocial personality disorder (APD) as "a pervasive pattern or disregard for, and violation of, the rights of others that begins in childhood or early adolescence and continues into adult-hood" (p. 701). There are two requirements for a diagnosis of APD: (a) must be 18 years or older, and (b) must have a documented history of a conduct disorder (CD) before the age of 15. CD is a serious psychiatric problem in young people that precedes APD. Older genetic research sug-gests that APD and CD are risk factors for alcoholism, but more likely these conditions involve earlier and heavier drinking (alcohol abuse), as opposed to a greater risk for alcohol dependence.

ADHD

Brereton (2010) describes ADHD as "a syndrome with core symptoms including difficulty maintaining attention, cognitive disorganization, distractibility, impulsivity, and hyperactivity. These symptoms, generally more common in boys, may vary between children and across differ-ent situations and times. Common secondary symptoms include percep-tual and emotional immaturity, poor social skills, disruptive behaviors, and academic problems." *DSM-IV-TR (2000)* describes three subtypes: ADHD, Combined Type (where both *inattention and hyperactivity-impul-sivity* are significant features); ADHD, Predominantly Inattentive Type (where the main feature is *inattentiveness*); and ADHD Predominantly Hyperactive-Impulsive Type (where the main feature is *hyperactivity*). While observers may see the symptoms as innocent and annoying nui-sances, most experts believe that left untreated, the ADHD symptoms will eventually interfere with the person's ability to mature and fully adjust to life's changes. Untreated ADHD is associated with the use of drugs later in life to reduce ADHD symptoms and is associated with an increased risk for alcohol dependence.

Other DSM Categories Relating to Drug Use

"Mental retardation" is an Axis II diagnostic category, and it is possible that when mentally retarded people abuse drugs, they may be trying to reduce symptoms of the disorder. Fetal alcohol spectrum disorder (FASD) is generally believed to be the most preventable form of mental retardation. The relationship between brain injuries (Axis III) and chemical dependence is a topic that needs more research, based upon the observation that brain injury and particularly PTSD seem to be related to an increased use of drugs and perhaps chemical dependence.

Psychotic States in Patients With Drug Use and Mental Disorders

There is often confusion as to what defines a hallucination, a delusion, and a misperception.

A hallucination is seeing, hearing, smelling, tasting, or feeling something that has no external stimulus or overt cause. An example is a person who is hearing voices yet no one is present or talking, or they see a person or animal standing before them, yet no person or animal is present. A delusion is a false belief that is resistant to reality testing. For example, a patient states, "I know that the newscaster on the television is personally talking to me" or a nonpregnant woman insists, "I am pregnant and having a baby in a few months." A misperception and an illusion are similar. A misperception is actually seeing, hearing, feeling, tasting, or touching some external stimulus, but misperceiving what it actually is or means. For example, a person in a drug-affected state may misperceive the presence of a large dog as a lion or bear, or when talking with a coworker, a person perceives the coworker is angry and interprets this as meaning the coworker is angry at him, when actually the coworker is angry from an argument at home with a spouse.

Individuals will have different levels of ego-strength and resilience. Ego-strength is a person's ability to maintain emotional and psychological stability, including a sense of identity and ability to cope with internal and external stress. It also determines the person's ability to tolerate criticism and rejection by others. People with low ego-strength tend to feel distress by experiencing confrontation, severe criticism, and rejection.

Many patients with co-occurring drug use and mental disorders will appear with ego-syntonic or ego-dystonic features, or both. When psychological qualities or traits (perceptions, interpretation patterns, thinking patterns) or psychiatric symptoms are ego-syntonic, they feel natural or normal to the person, even if these qualities and symptoms cause difficulties for others. When traits or symptoms are ego-syntonic, people do not tend to seek treatment, unless mandated. In contrast, the ego-dystonic person defines psychological qualities, traits, or symptoms that feel distressing and out of character. It is at this point that a person is usually willing to make efforts to seek treatment and make changes.

CHAPTER 3

Alcohol, the Drink of All Ages

PATIENTS' OVERVIEW

Ethanol, a colorless, water-soluble liquid also called drinking alcohol, has had a major effect on the history of the world. It is famous for its role in affecting the minds of humans, both poor and great. It is used in religious ceremonies, as a social lubricant, and for shutting down nerve cells that are firing too rapidly. In small daily doses, it also has beneficial effects on the heart and on the prevention of certain diseases. It alone has the power to unmask the causes of alcohol dependence, commonly known as alcoholism. It is so ubiquitous that children drink it in family gatherings, and it is also used to calm the elderly. In between, it is the cause of many deaths due to its toxicity on major organs such as the liver, and from car crashes when people drink and drive. It is the primary beverage drunk during the Super Bowl. Sadly, it is also a part of spectator sports of all kinds, and society has still not found a way to control its negative effects.

Pharmacologists prefer to classify drugs that produce use disorders on their central nervous system (CNS) pharmacological effects and to include legal drugs such as alcohol, caffeine, and nicotine.

1. Alcohol (the most common social drug, and a depressant with early stimulant effects),
2. CNS stimulants (cocaine, amphetamines, caffeine, antidepressants),

3. CNS depressants (opioids, benzodiazepines, barbiturates),
4. CNS drugs used by adolescents [nicotine (tobacco), marijuana (cannabis), prescription drugs, steroids, club drugs, inhalants, abused over-the-counter drugs]

Alcohol

Alcohol (ethyl alcohol, ethanol, grain alcohol) is created when foods ferment, such as grains (e.g., wheat), fruits (e.g., grapes), or vegetables (e.g., potatoes). Fermentation (usually performed by yeast) is a process by which sugars are oxidized to ethanol and carbon dioxide. In bread making, the alcohol is baked out. In the production of beverage alcohols, the carbon dioxide is released into the atmosphere or used in carbonating the beverage.

Three other important alcohols exist: methyl alcohol (methanol, a.k.a. wood alcohol), isopropyl alcohol (isopropanol, a.k.a. rubbing alcohol), and butyl alcohol (butanol). Methyl alcohol is sometimes used as an antifreeze, solvent, fuel, or a denaturant for ethanol. The drinking of a small amount (such as 2 teaspoons) can cause permanent blindness, and about 6 teaspoons are potentially lethal. Isopropyl alcohol, as well as ethyl alcohol (often denatured), is used in many types of rubbing alcohols. The ingestion of isopropyl alcohol will cause severe headache, gastric upset, and nausea. Finally, n-butyl alcohol is found in tiny amounts in alcoholic beverages (as "fusel alcohols") and is also present in small quantities in foods and consumer products.

Blood Alcohol Concentration

Ethanol is the alcohol found in beverages such as beer, wine, and spirits. One standard beverage unit is one 12-oz bottle of beer, one 5-oz glass of wine, one cocktail containing 1.5 oz of spirits, or an equivalent of any of the above. All of these contain about 14 g of absolute alcohol (ethanol). For beverages containing more or less alcohol than in a standard beverage unit, only slight differences will be seen from the calculations for alcohol in the blood in the following examples. For example, a "light" beer produces similar blood alcohol levels as a "regular" beer for purposes of blood alcohol concentration (BAC).

For an "average" 150-pound (68-kilogram) male drinking one beverage unit in an hour, the result will be a BAC of 0.025%. A 200-pound (91-kilogram) male would have a BAC of 0.019% under the same conditions. Because the U.S. national driving while intoxicated (DWI) legal limit is 0.08%, it is easy to calculate that the average male would have to drink about four drinks in an hour to reach the DWI limit. During that hour, his body would break down (metabolize) an amount of alcohol that produces a BAC of 0.02% (average metabolism for most people). Thus four drinks in an hour would produce a BAC of 0.10% minus 0.02% metabolism during the hour of consumption = 0.08% (the DWI limit). (Note: Most people do not drink four drinks in an hour, but experienced drinkers often do.)

Because women metabolize less alcohol in the gastrointestinal tract, and because of a fat/water ratio that is different from that of men, one drink will produce a higher BAC in women than in men. So for a 150-pound (68-kilogram) woman, each standard drink per hour would produce a BAC of 0.03%. Thus, three drinks in an hour would produce almost the 0.08% drink-driving legal limit (0.03% x 3 = 0.09% minus 0.02% metabolism in an hour = 0.07%.) Of course, other factors would affect the final BAC and the observed level of "intoxication" in both men and women. Among the factors that can influence the level of intoxication are genetics, drinking history, amount of food in the stomach, rate of drinking, presence of other drugs that affect alcohol metabolism, overall health of the individual, and the natural tolerance to alcohol. Natural tolerance to alcohol is seen when, for example, a person drinks 3 pints (1.4 liters) of beer (equal to four standard drinks) in an hour and shows no effect. Such people have been called "low responders" to alcohol, and it appears this is a genetic trait that relates to a greater risk for alcohol dependence later in life. The genetic trait somehow is expressed in differences in liver enzymes that metabolize alcohol, altered brain sensitivity to alcohol, and other as yet unknown factors. ("High responders" to alcohol have not been studied scientifically, but might best be seen when one standard drink puts a person to sleep.)

Signs of Intoxication

Visible signs of intoxication include decreased inhibitions and psychomotor or cognitive impairment such as the following:

- Being boisterous, argumentative, confrontational, obnoxious, or annoying; acting silly
- Exhibiting slow, slurred, mumbled, or incoherent speech; staggering, stumbling, or holding on to objects for balance; putting head on bar or sleeping at the bar; bumping into objects or people while walking; using exaggerated hand or arm gestures; spilling food or drinks; losing balance
- Giving a delayed response to questions; giving illogical comments or answers to questions; having impaired memory;

lighting the wrong end of a cigarette; being excessively quiet or sullen; being in denial of impaired driving ability; having trouble counting money; having difficulty following instructions or directions.

A legal definition of "obvious intoxication" is often used in court cases in which plaintiffs allege that bartenders and waitstaff should be aware that some patrons in an establishment might be too intoxicated to drive an automobile. Indeed, many bars and restaurants have been convicted of overserving patrons who later were involved in crashes that were caused by high blood alcohol levels. What is "obvious intoxication"? In many states, obvious intoxication is defined as "visible intoxication," in which customers show visible signs of intoxication that should be apparent to bartenders and witnesses (Brick & Erickson, 2009).

In those cases where bartenders, waitstaff, and witnesses did not see any of the above signs, other states have allowed the counting of drinks to be evidence of obvious intoxication, when properly trained employees should have been able to monitor the number of drinks sold or given to customers. After all, they say, the consequences of drunk driving are far too serious for bars and restaurants to absolve themselves from the practice of overserving customers. A critical question to be decided in all such cases is the proportion of responsibility held by the customer in overdrinking and the proportion held by the establishment in overserving an intoxicated customer who may be impaired in making decisions about continuing to drink.

On a continuum of drinking, we can define terms such as *social drinking, moderate drinking, binge drinking, heavy drinking, problem drinking, risky drinking, unhealthy drinking, alcohol abuse, alcoholism,* and *alcohol dependence*. Briefly, *social drinking* is the occasional use of alcohol, such as having a cold beer (or two) after a workout, or drinking a glass of wine (or two) with a meal. *Moderate drinking* is one to two drinks per day (one for women, two for men) and has been related to benefits such as a reduction in heart disease. *Binge drinking* is defined by researchers as five drinks in one sitting (although nonresearchers can imagine that a night of heavy drinking is also a binge). *Heavy drinking* includes a range of drinking as defined by number of drinks and duration of drinking. The range is from five glasses of wine (for example) per day (24 hr) to unlimited drinks. Note: The definition of *heavy* in this instance is in the eye of the beholder and is not scientific. For example, a pint of tequila drunk in an hour is surely heavy drinking, but what about a 12-pack of light beer at a tailgating party over the course of a football game? (For gender and cultural differences in drinking outcomes, see Chapter 9.)

Any situation where drinking alcohol (usually over a period of weeks or months) causes physical, psychological, or social consequences in the drinker is called *problem drinking*. This is the type of drinking recognized by 12-step programs as what characterizes an individual as an "alcoholic." *Risky drinking* is a relatively new term in that it has been recognized by the American Medical Association as something that physicians must become familiar with. Risky drinking means drinking at levels that put a person at risk of medical or social problems. For men this means more than 14 drinks per week, or more than four drinks on any occasion. For women this means more than seven drinks per week or more than three drinks on any occasion.

Unhealthy drinking is a general term that encompasses all of the preceding terms except social and moderate drinking. *Alcohol abuse* generally is synonymous with the terms *binge drinking, heavy drinking, problem drinking, risky drinking,* and *unhealthy drinking,* and current *DSM-IV-TR (2000)* criteria help to diagnose individuals who are alcohol abusers. (Note: The term *abuse* will not appear in the next edition, *DSM-V,* due to be published in 2013.) *Alcoholism* is the disease described by AA and is closest to the term *problem drinking* as defined above. However, scientists studying alcoholism realize that the more accurate scientific term is *alcohol dependence,* which can be diagnosed using contemporary *DSM-IV-TR (2000)* criteria describing the brain disease in which individuals cannot control their drinking.

Metabolism of Alcohol

The breakdown (metabolism) of alcohol is important in many ways. First, metabolism causes alcohol to disappear from the blood and eventually from the body. The liver is the main site of metabolism, where enzymes cause ethanol to be converted to acetaldehyde. The main enzyme that does this is alcohol dehydrogenase. In turn, acetaldehyde is broken down (by aldehyde dehydrogenase) into carbon dioxide and water. Acetaldehyde is part of the cause of hangovers. It is also the metabolite that makes some Asian individuals sensitive to alcohol by preventing them from breaking down alcohol adequately; because of the acetaldehyde accumulation in the body, some Asian individuals become flushed and ill, which usually reduces their desire to drink. The drug Antabuse (disulfiram) is used to dissuade alcohol abusers (such as repeat DWI offenders) from drinking, through court-ordered prescriptions. Antabuse significantly slows the aldehyde dehydrogenase enzyme, causing a buildup of acetaldehyde and its unpleasant consequences.

Alcohol consumption can be monitored by blood tests (the most accurate), breathalyzers, and sweat and urine measures. Blood tests and breathalyzers are both qualitative (they specifically measure the presence of alcohol) and quantitative (they accurately measure the amount of alcohol). Urine tests are qualitative and somewhat quantitative (although undependable), and sweat tests are only qualitative. Through known parameters of metabolism and distribution of alcohol, scientists can measure alcohol in blood, breath, sweat, and urine; as a result, experts are able to calculate the BAC at the time of an accident or at the time of death. (Acetaldehyde is not useful in this regard because it cannot easily be measured in the blood.)

Beneficial Effects of Alcohol Use

The social and moderate use of beverage alcohol rarely causes untoward effects. In fact, the social use of alcohol has positive effects, such as relaxation, enhancement of socialization, and even the facilitating of sleep (especially in the elderly). Older allegations of alcohol's ability to increase digestion, cure colds, reduce Alzheimer's disease, or reduce pain and anxiety are less studied than the negative effects of alcohol. Alcohol is used therapeutically in nerve blocks, where the anesthetic action of alcohol can temporarily reduce nerve cell function, as in severe pain conditions such as trigeminal neuralgia. Also, there is an impressive body of research showing that moderate drinking can reduce the incidence of ischemic stroke and cardiovascular disease involving cholesterol buildup in arteries, or via a blood-thinning effect. There is also evidence that the social activity of consuming alcohol may reduce the incidence of cardiovascular disease. Whereas with heavy drinking ethanol clearly damages heart muscle (leading to more heart attacks), the mechanism of reducing heart attacks with social drinking appears to involve the prevention of coronary plaques. Other beneficial effects of social drinking, although more controversial, include prevention of gallstones and kidney stones, reduced risk of Type 2 diabetes, and reduced risk of dementia.

Negative Effects of Alcohol Use

Some of the beneficial effects of social drinking can encourage people to drink more. When people have impulse control problems, they may drink more than intended and end up with the conditions of problem drinking, alcohol abuse, and alcohol dependence. Especially when one hears that alcohol is good for one's heart, the natural tendency is to think, "More is better." But the beneficial effects of alcohol are clearly restricted to mild to moderate consumption (i.e., two drinks per day for men and one drink per day for women).

Other negative effects of alcohol include the following: increases in the incidence of fatty liver and cirrhosis, increased cancer risk (pancreas, mouth, pharynx, larynx, esophagus, bowel, liver, breast), pancreatitis, stroke, high blood pressure, miscarriage, gastritis, injuries due to impaired motor skills (e.g., drunk driving), suicide, memory lapses under the influence (a.k.a. blackouts), depression, increased sexual desire combined with reduced sexual performance, altered appetite for food, and fetal alcohol spectrum disorder (FASD). Because alcohol produces "dose-related effects," the above negative effects are related to higher levels of drinking, greater frequency of drinking, more drinking days, and (perhaps genetic) differences in vulnerability to certain alcohol-induced symptoms and diseases. Of course, some of the negative effects of alcohol have received more scientific attention (e.g., liver problems) than others (e.g., stroke).

FASD
FASD is one of the more notable side effects of heavy drinking in pregnant females who are predisposed to negatively affecting their babies with alcohol. FASD is a new term (encompassing the severe fetal alcohol syndrome [FAS] and less serious fetal alcohol effects [FAE]) that describes the range of adverse effects on the baby of drinking during pregnancy. About 1 in 1,000 women who drink heavily during pregnancy will have a child with full-blown FAS: a permanent syndrome. A baby with FAS has a small head; defects of the hands, feet, kidneys, and brain; low IQ; and characteristic signs of the problem in the face: wide-set eyes, missing filtrum (raised portion between the nose and upper lip), thin lips, and flat facial characteristics. Women who drink only during certain trimesters of pregnancy may have babies with some of these characteristics but not all. Women who drink in moderation or sporadically during pregnancy may have children with a few of these characteristics that are milder (FAE) than those seen in FAS. Children born with FAS have extraordinary needs, such as counseling, special education and parenting attention, and long-term attention. The prognosis for children with FAS is poor; therefore, much of the current research in this area focuses on prevention: education of pregnant mothers about the effects of drinking on the fetus, and treatment of pregnant alcohol-dependent women and adolescents.

Underage Drinking
Although alcohol is illegal to consume under the age of 21 in the United States, underage drinking is a big problem. Adolescents and young adults can be exposed to alcohol through parents, peers, and others in their group who are over 21. College underage drinking is particularly problematic when students of different ages live together, study together,

and attend athletic events together. Underage drinking is so pervasive that law enforcement tends to ignore the problem, unless the person gets into trouble with a minor in possession (MIP) or driving under the influence (DUI), or the more serious charge of driving while intoxicated (DWI). One of the major problems with trying to prevent drinking in young people is that there is major peer acceptance and even peer pressure to drink. In addition, neurobiologists have found that the brain's frontal lobes, where judgment, decision making, and impulse control reside, do not fully develop until about the age of between 20 and 24. Thus, prevention messages given to adolescents and young adults (18–22 years of age) are heard, processed, but often not acted upon because the brains of many adolescents and young adults are not fully capable of making proper decisions based upon good judgment. In addition, lack of impulse control usually drives the drinking behavior, even though the person knows better. In general, adolescent drinking and even progression to alcohol dependence and its treatment have all been understudied by scientists so far. More research on this important topic needs to be carried out in the future.

Alcohol research in the United States is primarily funded by the National Institutes of Health (NIH), especially the National Institute on Alcohol Abuse and Alcoholism (NIAAA). ABMRF/The Foundation for Alcohol Research also funds some work, particularly with start-up funds for promising new investigators at academic and scientific institutions in Canada and the United States. In the United Kingdom, the Alcohol Education and Research Council funds small and large grants for the improvement of practitioner and research skills in the alcohol field, as well as studentship grants to encourage research in the alcohol field.

CHAPTER 4

Alcohol and Drug Interactions

with Mark Evan Goldman, PhD

PATIENTS' OVERVIEW

Because alcohol is a drug that is legally available and used by most members of society (except those under 21 years of age), and because many people take prescription medications, it is important for people to understand that many medications can interact (mostly in a negative way) with alcohol. These interactions range from a relatively mild change in medication effectiveness (as when taken with antibiotics) to major interactions that can threaten life (as when taken with a benzodiazepine). For "alcoholics," of course, any medication that contains alcohol or that can affect mood might cause a relapse.

Interactions of medications (Drug A and Drug B) with drugs of abuse can affect the "amount" of either Drug A or Drug B in the blood (and therefore the target organs such as the brain); this is called a "pharmacokinetic interaction." For example, antacids, which are commonly used to treat stomach acidity, will decrease blood levels of many antibiotics, such as ciprofloxacin (Cipro). Conversely, the presence of Drug A and Drug B can also affect the "action" of Drug A and/or Drug B on the target organs such as the brain. This effect is called a "pharmacodynamic interaction." Numerous medications listed below increase the sedating effects of alcohol through a pharmacodynamic interaction. These are the major interactions of drugs with alcohol.

For a complete list of prescription medications that interact with alcohol, see: http://pubs.niaaa.nih.gov/publications/medicine/medicine.htm

Alcohol Alone

Before discussing interactions of alcohol with other drugs, some brief statements about the chemical nature of alcohols are warranted. Many alcohols have industrial and scientific uses but ethanol is the most commonly used form of alcohol for human consumption and is referred to simply as "alcohol" in this book. Other chemical alcohols are extremely toxic to many organs, especially the liver. Alcohol is typically drunk recreationally (Chapter 3), but it has other uses. Even recently (the earthquake disaster in Haiti, 2010), concentrated alcohol beverages were used to sterilize a patient's skin before "field" surgeries. Unlike most other drugs of abuse that are given in milligram doses, alcohol is not very potent (i.e., it is a weakly active drug), with about 14 g of alcohol consumed in the average bar drink serving. Although alcohol is termed a "drug" for this book, rare therapeutic (medicinal) uses do exist, but typically as a last resort; for example, concentrated alcohol is injected into the nerves of the sympathetic ganglia to treat long-lasting pain caused by inoperable cancer and trigeminal neuralgia. Parenteral (injectable) ethanol is used to treat poisoning by other alcohols as well as poisoning by ethylene glycol (antifreeze). Finally, alcohol historically was used, but is no longer recommended, for obstetrical procedures to slow down delivery.

Following acute consumption of alcohol beverages, there are several behavioral stages of alcohol including an initial stimulant phase and a later somnolent phase. The combination of alcohol with medications and drugs, therefore, can enhance the effects of either type of medication. Labels on medications often (but not always) caution against concomitant use with alcohol.

Alcohol and Benzodiazepine Sedatives

Alcohol in combination with benzodiazepine sedatives is dangerous because the sedating properties of alcohol and benzodiazepines are significantly enhanced, more fully reducing coordination. Together, these agents slow down motor function, including respiration. Examples of these heightened pharmacodynamic interactions include effects on walking, driving, verbal communication, memory for events, and a potential for enhanced levels of crime (date rape, robbery). In some people, paradoxical effects (aggression, violence, impulsivity, and suicidal behavior) are caused by either of these agents, and this paradoxical effect may be further enhanced when the two drugs are combined. Similarly, the combination may result in greater expression of depressive and suicidal tendencies. Neither alcohol nor benzodiazepines are indicated for use during pregnancy due to teratogenic effects (fetal malformation), and obviously combining them in pregnant women is never recommended. With any use of benzodiazepines, adding alcohol is more dangerous because the amnesic effects of each are added together, potentially resulting in overconsumption of one or both agents.

Due to enhanced effects on the respiratory system, the combination of alcohol with benzodiazepines is contraindicated in people with myasthenia gravis, sleep apnea, or chronic obstructive pulmonary disease. Because the acute effects of each drug on the brain are similar, chronic administration of alcohol with the acute or chronic use of benzodiazepines can potentiate each of the drug effects. For example, people using alcohol chronically may have a decreased ability to metabolize benzodiazepines in the liver, resulting in increased levels in the blood. Therefore, there are greater effects of both benzodiazepines and alcohol (pharmacokinetic interaction). Each drug depresses respiratory function and, in combination, there are greater risks to breathing (pharmacodynamic interaction).

Alcohol is cross-tolerant with benzodiazepines (as well as with barbiturates), meaning that when a person becomes tolerant to alcohol (needs more and more to produce the same original effect), there is some buildup of tolerance to the other drugs, even when the other drugs have not been used. This is due to the enhancement of similar liver enzymes that break down alcohol and the other drugs. Similarly, people tolerant to benzodiazepines can build up tolerance to alcohol. Finally, different benzodiazepines are cross-tolerant with each other, which is the reason that long-acting benzodiazepines can be used to detoxify short-acting benzodiazepine–dependent patients.

Alcohol and Antihistamines

Diphenhydramine (Benadryl) is used to treat symptoms of seasonal and perennial allergies, insomnia, and travel-related motion sickness. Therapeutically, its mechanism of action is to block histamine (H1) receptors, although it also dose-dependently interacts (directly or indirectly) with many other receptor systems including acetylcholine, serotonin, noradrenergic, dopamine, opioid, and adenosine. Through these mechanisms, it produces gastrointestinal and antiemetic effects and, notably, sedative effects. Therefore, as with all sedative medications, combinations with alcohol are potentially very dangerous due to enhanced sedative properties.

Alcohol and Stimulants

"Stimulant" is a wide category of pharmacologic substances that includes freely available agents like coffee, tobacco, and sports drinks; "behind the pharmacy-counter medications" like pseudoephedrine; prescription medications such as amphetamine dispensed by a pharmacist; and clandestine-lab-synthesized drugs like "speed," methylenedioxymethamphetamine (MDMA, ecstasy) and cocaine. As medications, stimulants are used to treat a variety of cognitive and physical conditions such as fatigue in shift-work sleep disorder, to decrease appetite, to improve focus in individuals with attention deficit/hyperactivity disorder (ADHD), and to treat clinical depression. However, with chronic and high-dose administration they can also induce "stimulant psychosis." In addition to its stimulant properties, cocaine is an ophthalmic (eye) anesthetic. In fact, television and movies show people placing "white powder" on their gums to determine if the "cocaine-like" substance has topical anesthetic properties.

An old wives' tale is that coffee can be used to help an intoxicated person. This only produces an agitated, alert, yet intoxicated person. This has been found to be false in scientific studies examining alcohol-induced impairment of human performance. Similarly, no stimulants scientifically improve performance of depressant-intoxicated people. Conversely, chronic alcoholics may have a reduced ability to metabolize stimulants and their combined use may pose a greater health risk due to increased blood pressure and nervousness. When used in large quantities, stimulants increase psychopathology in the form of anxiety, rebound depression, agitation, and restlessness. The classic use of a strong stimulant offset by a strong depressant has many risks, too. Strong alcohol sedation that occurs along with the exhaustion/depression from stimulant withdrawal can lead to a serious depression of the cardiorespiratory system, especially in weak and compromised patients.

Alcohol and Antibiotics

In healthy people, alcohol is rapidly absorbed into the blood from the stomach and small intestines, although the speed can vary if the person has an empty or full stomach. Once inside the body, alcohol is removed mostly by liver metabolism, although elimination from the breath, urine, and sweat also occurs. In people with alcoholic cirrhosis of the liver, metabolism of alcohol is greatly impaired.

Ciprofloxacin (Cipro) is a common oral broad-spectrum antibiotic that is used frequently to treat both aerobic and anaerobic infections. Ciprofloxacin administration to humans at a "clinical dose" (750 mg twice daily) reduces alcohol elimination by 9%, thereby extending the duration of alcohol's actions. In patients with reduced liver function this effect is magnified. These situations emphasize the importance of paying attention to labels on medication bottles and the counseling given to patients by pharmacists.

Alcohol and Tobacco Interactions

The observation that tobacco use increases a desire to drink in greater amounts has been observed for at least two centuries, with Benjamin Rush, a physician and signer of the Declaration of Independence, citing this concern. The observation that tobacco use increases a desire to use alcohol and other drugs has been widely observed by addiction treatment practitioners for decades. Researchers have found that even small amounts of alcohol boost the pleasurable effects of nicotine, inducing people to smoke more when drinking alcoholic beverages. The 2005 National Survey on Drug Use and Health noted that tobacco had a reinforcing effect and enhanced the effects of alcohol and cocaine. Furthermore, an association was found with binge drinking (43.8% of current cigarette users vs. 15.7% of current nonusers) and heavy drinking (16.1% vs. 3.5%, respectively). Finally, it appears alcohol and tobacco use increases the risk of illness over time. The disease-related morbidity, specifically for lung, mouth, and throat cancers, has been consistently much higher for those who smoke and use alcohol heavily as compared to those who use only one or the other.

Hidden Alcohol and Medication Interactions

It is important for those people in treatment for alcoholism or in 12-step programs to understand that any mood-altering chemical (excluding antidepressants, antipsychotics, and antimania drugs, which are not "mood altering") has the potential to produce a relapse. However, the use of alcohol with many psychiatric drugs, including antidepressants and neuroleptics, can result in severe additive depressant effects and can be fatal. This includes prescription and over-the-counter medications that contain alcohol (such as some cough and cold remedies and liquid vitamin preparations). Any medication containing drugs that cause sedation (e.g., antiallergy medications), prescription painkillers (especially OxyContin and morphine), and sleep aids (e.g., doxylamine) are particularly risky. It is important for someone in treatment to be truthful with his or her physician, nurse, or pharmacist about treatment for alcohol abstinence so that there is a lower likelihood that medications will be used that produce a risk of relapse.

Conclusions

As the number of elderly people increases across societies, attention should also be given to the effects of alcohol and medicine interactions as a function of age. There is a correlation between increasing age and increasing use of medications and the effects of medications can be significantly enhanced or diminished even with small doses of alcohol. As a result, medical care providers should be aware of all medications being taken by patients to reduce the chances of adverse effects of combined medication use.

CHAPTER 5

Drugs That Speed Us Up

PATIENTS' OVERVIEW

Cocaine has been used for centuries and amphetamines have been known for decades for their ability to stimulate the brain. People on these drugs feel a special "high," which in some cases is very pleasant and in other cases can become dangerous. The "high" is caused generally by an increase in the release of dopamine in the brain"s reward (pleasure) pathway. When these drugs are used for their therapeutic effect, they work very well. When these drugs are abused, however, the long-term effects are less than pleasant. In some people, these drugs can cause chemical dependence, by producing a dysregulation of the dopamine system. Caffeine, a mild stimulant used for millennia, can be overused but has not yet equivocally been shown to produce chemical dependence.

There are many ways to classify illegal and prescription drugs that cause use disorders and "addiction." The Drug Enforcement Administration (DEA), through the Controlled Substances Act (CSA), classifies drugs into five schedules—I, II, III, IV, and V—based upon their abuse potential. Drugs in Schedule I are highly abused but have no accepted therapeutic use (e.g., heroin). Drugs in the other four schedules are abused and have accepted therapeutic uses. Drugs in Schedule II have the highest abuse liability among therapeutic classes (e.g., methadone). Drugs in Schedule III have less abuse liability than those in Schedule II (e.g., anabolic steroids). Drugs in Schedule IV have less abuse liability than those in Schedule III (e.g., phenobarbital). Finally, drugs in Schedule V have less abuse liability than those in Schedule IV (e.g., low doses of codeine). The purpose of the CSA is to classify drugs for the purpose of their control and the punishment of users and distributors of the listed drugs.

In contrast, the United Kingdom classifies illegal drugs into three classes—Classes A, B, and C (HomeOffice.gov.uk, 2010). Class A drugs have the highest penalty for possession (7 years in prison or an unlimited fine or both), and for dealing (up to life in prison or an unlimited fine or both). Drugs in this class include ecstasy, LSD, heroin, cocaine, crack, magic mushrooms, and injectable amphetamines. Class B drugs include amphetamines, cannabis, and methylphenidate (Ritalin). The prison time for this class ranges from 5 years (possession) to 14 years (dealing). Finally, Class C drugs include tranquilizers, some painkillers, GHB, and ketamine, for which a person can serve up to 2 years (possession) or up to 14 years (dealing). All of the drugs are designated controlled substances under the Misuse of Drugs Act of 1971. Class A drugs are perceived to be the most likely to cause harm.

Both of the above listings are administrative ways to classify drugs based upon their harm, legality, and types of punishment for possession and dealing.

Central Stimulants

In certain diseases and conditions, specific areas of the brain have a tendency to slow down. For example, shift workers (e.g., police officers, flight controllers) have a difficult time maintaining normal patterns of sleep when a shift is changed. In clinical depression or dysthymia there is an apparent malaise and lack of appreciation of everyday events that should make us happy: birthday parties, weddings, a gentle kiss, or a smile from a friend. Or we may be too tired, and just can't get out of bed or work on that chore that's been on the list for a week. In other conditions, one part of the brain speeds up and makes it difficult to concentrate (as in anxiety). As another example, one part of the brain runs slow or is less mature, causing the "brakes" to be taken off other brain areas, leading to increased activity (as in attention deficit/hyperactivity disorder [ADHD]).

Central nervous system (CNS) stimulants, then, are capable of stimulating a normal brain or a diseased/decompensated one. Amphetamines are the drugs of choice in treating ADHD, and they work paradoxically by boosting the activity of a part of the frontal lobes to put the brakes on other brain areas that are running too fast. The main neurotransmitter involved in this therapeutic action is the one that most people have heard about: dopamine. Dopamine is one of those rare transmitters that can either excite nerves or depress nerves, depending on the brain area where it is in action. In the case of ADHD, dopamine is clearly stimulatory and it enhances the activity of a frontal lobe area that is underdeveloped in ADHD. The normal function of the brain area is to balance other brain areas that control concentration, behavior, and motor (muscle) activity.

Cocaine and caffeine are strong and mild stimulants, respectively, that are primarily used for their ability to increase people's pleasure and concentration. Coca leaves, from which cocaine is derived, are routinely chewed by South American natives for the mild stimulant effect they produce. Caffeine, a mild stimulant, is the main ingredient in social drinks such as coffee, tea, and sodas. Cocaine as a stimulant is illegal; caffeine is legal. Let's take a look at each of these drugs, in turn.

The stimulant, abuse, and dependence-producing effects of CNS stimulants are well known. For a full description, an excellent pharmacology book for the general public is titled *Buzzed*, by Kuhn, Swartzwelder, and Wilson (2008). InfoFacts, published online by the National Institute on Drug Abuse, is another good source of facts about CNS stimulants.

Cocaine

Cocaine is a powerfully addicting (dependence-producing) drug that directly affects the brain. It is one of the oldest known drugs, having been abused for more than a century. Coca leaves, from which cocaine is extracted, have been used by native peoples for thousands of years as a mild stimulant for recreation and to enhance mood. Although cocaine is used therapeutically and legally as a local anesthetic before eye surgery, it is most known for its illegal uses by people using the drug recreationally. Because it is legal, it is classified as a Schedule II drug and therefore its availability for use is strictly controlled by the DEA. Most illegal use of cocaine occurs as a result of the illegal import, sale, and distribution of the drug.

The two chemical forms of cocaine that are abused are the water-soluble cocaine hydrochloride salt and the water-insoluble cocaine base (or freebase, which has the salt removed). When abused, the hydrochloride salt, or powdered form of cocaine, can be injected or snorted. When the hydrochloride salt is mixed with ammonia or sodium bicarbonate (baking soda) and water, and then heated to remove the hydrochloride, a smokable substance ("freebase") is formed. Further processing produces "crack," the street name given to processed freebase cocaine. "Crack" refers to the crackling sound heard when the mixture is smoked. Smoking produces a rapid high when cocaine is absorbed into the blood through the lungs, as rapidly as by intravenous injection. Regardless of the method of cocaine use, all routes can lead to dependence production and other severe health problems, such as an increase in the risk of contracting HIV and other infectious diseases through needle sharing.

Injecting or smoking cocaine produces a quicker, stronger high than snorting. Conversely, faster absorption usually means a shorter duration of action: The high from snorting cocaine may last 15–30 min, but the high from smoking may last only 5–10 min. Cocaine produces its effects on the brain's reward pathway by increasing the levels of dopamine, the neurotransmitter associated with pleasure and movement. The excess levels of dopamine underlie cocaine's euphoric effects. With repeated use, cocaine can cause long-term changes in the brain's reward pathway and also in other brain areas, and it is these changes that are thought to lead to chemical dependence.

Cocaine constricts blood vessels, dilates pupils, and increases body temperature, heart rate, and blood pressure. It can also produce headaches and abdominal pain and nausea. Because cocaine (as well as amphetamines) tends to decrease appetite, chronic users can lose significant amounts of body weight. Regular snorting of cocaine through the nose can cause local anesthesia and can lead to a loss of the sense of smell, nosebleeds, problems with swallowing, hoarseness, and a chronically runny nose. More dramatically, the chronic snorting of cocaine constricts nasal passages for so long that the nasal septum becomes ruptured. Regardless of the route or frequency of use, cocaine abusers can experience heart attack or stroke, which may cause sudden death. If cocaine users also consume alcohol, the risk of problems can markedly increase through the liver's production of a cocaine-ethanol metabolite called cocaethylene. Cocaethylene intensifies cocaine's euphoric effects, and perhaps the risk of sudden death.

Cocaine dependence is more difficult to treat than dependence on other drugs, presumably because of the intense euphoria produced by cocaine and the emotional memory connected to this effect. Unfortunately, there are no consistently effective medications that work to reduce craving for cocaine, so the treatment options are mostly behavioral. Behavioral interventions, such as cognitive behavioral therapy (CBT), have been shown to be effective in decreasing cocaine use and preventing relapse. Most successful treatments involve a combination of behavioral therapy, social support, and other services. One promising therapy involves a cocaine vaccine, which would bind to cocaine in the blood and prevent it from crossing the blood-brain barrier to exert its effects.

Cocaine use and abuse is significant among Americans. Survey figures from 2008 (SAMHSA, 2009) indicate that almost 36 million Americans aged 12 and older have used cocaine, and about 8.6 million have used crack. An estimated 2.1 million Americans had used cocaine in the previous month, whereas over 610,000 were current users of crack. Among young adults aged 18–25, past-year use was 6.4% (SAMHSA, 2009). About 17% of cocaine users and about 20% of crack users, develop cocaine dependence (the disease of "addiction," Table 1.1).

The U.S. War on Drugs has traditionally focused on preventing drugs from reaching the users. Thus, interdiction activities on the seas and at the borders are trumpeted in news stories for their success in blocking drug shipments and bringing down drug lords in charge of cartels that facilitate large amounts of drugs getting to Americans. However, the United States is slowly changing that strategy to include more emphasis on reducing the demand for drugs: drug prevention campaigns, treatment for drug users to reduce the need for drugs, and education of the public about the dangers of drugs. At the very least, a combination of demand reduction and reducing the supply is needed to begin the long process of reducing illegal drug use in the United States.

Amphetamines

Amphetamines as a class are stimulant prescription drugs that act similarly to cocaine, with the following differences:

- The primary route of amphetamines ingestion is orally, although, like cocaine, they can also be smoked (inhaled by mouth), injected, or snorted (inhaled through the nose). These last three routes are primarily used when these drugs are taken illegally, for they produce the fastest and most powerful euphoric high.
- A dose of cocaine generally lasts for a shorter period of time than a dose of amphetamine taken by the same route.
- There are many amphetamines, some of which are used for therapeutic purposes; there is only one cocaine medication, albeit it comes in different forms for usage.
- Cocaine is a naturally occurring chemical, whereas amphetamines are synthetic.
- Cocaine increases dopamine in the brain by blocking its transport into the releasing cells; amphetamines increase dopamine,

serotonin, and norepinephrine by increasing their release from the cells.

Amphetamines have therapeutic uses in the treatment of ADHD, narcolepsy, and chronic fatigue syndrome. When used properly for therapeutic purposes, these drugs rarely cause euphoria and usually are not abused. In the past, amphetamines were used to reduce appetite for weight control, but now are felt to have too many side effects, including abuse and chemical dependence, for this indication. Popular amphetamine drugs include Adderall, Dexedrine, and (in the past) Benzedrine. These drugs act in the brain's reward pathway to produce a euphoric high, much like cocaine. Thus, chronic amphetamine abuse can also lead to chemical dependence. For this reason, the amphetamine drugs are listed in Schedule II of the CSA.

The most abused amphetamine, methamphetamine, is a prototype of this class of CNS stimulants. Most of the abused methamphetamine in the United States comes from foreign or domestic superlabs. However, it can also be made in small, illegal laboratories that are reminiscent of the illegal "stills" for alcohol during U.S. prohibition. In small labs, methamphetamine production endangers the people in the labs, their neighbors, and the environment.

Chronic methamphetamine abuse significantly changes how the brain functions. Brain imaging studies have shown alterations in the dopamine systems of humans that are associated with reduced motor skills and impaired verbal learning. Recent studies in the chronic users have also shown severe structural and functional changes in areas of the brain related to emotion and memory. Such changes might account for many of the emotional and cognitive problems seen in chronic methamphetamine users.

Side effects of amphetamine use are increased wakefulness, increased physical activity, decreased appetite, increased respiration, rapid heart rate, irregular heartbeat, increased blood pressure, and elevated body temperature. Long-term amphetamine use can cause extreme weight loss, severe dental problems ("meth mouth"), anxiety, confusion, insomnia, mood disturbances, and violent behavior. In addition, there may be psychotic symptoms (paranoia, visual and auditory hallucinations, and delusions), causing some to think that these drugs work on the same brain areas as those that cause the symptoms of schizophrenia.

As with cocaine, there are no medications available for the treatment of amphetamine dependence. Thus this addiction is difficult to treat. The most effective treatment for amphetamine dependence is comprehensive CBT. For example, the Matrix model at UCLA has been shown to be effective in reducing amphetamine dependence. This model involves a treatment approach combining behavioral therapy, family education, individual counseling, 12-step support, drug testing, and encouragement for non-drug-related activities.

Amphetamine abuse (including abuse of Adderall and methylphenidate, Ritalin) has leveled off and even declined somewhat in the United States. Stimulant abuse is due to high school and college students using amphetamines, often obtained from peers who are using the drug with legitimate prescriptions, or obtained on the black market. For methamphetamine, the number of individuals aged 12 or older reporting past-year use is around 0.5 million (SAMHSA, 2009). About 0.2% of the American population was past-month users. About 11% of those who use amphetamines will develop amphetamine dependence (Table 1.1). In general, students need information about the disadvantages of using prescription drugs as an aid to studying and to taking exams.

Caffeine

Compared to cocaine and amphetamines, caffeine is very mild and very safe. The National Institute on Drug Abuse does not even name it in its list of dangerous drugs, yet it may be the most popular drug (in addition to alcohol) in the world. Caffeine is found in coffee, tea, cocoa, chocolate, some soft drinks, and some over-the-counter drugs (such as Vivarin and NoDoz). The natural sources of caffeine are the coffee bean, tea leaf, kola nut, and cacao pod. Contrary to popular belief, tea only has about one third to one half the amount of caffeine as compared to coffee, but tea has a chemical cousin called theophylline. Theophylline has some cardiac stimulation effects, and was once used in asthma and chronic obstructive pulmonary disease (COPD) medications to help improve breathing.

Pure caffeine is odorless and has a bitter taste. In moderate doses (100–200 mg), caffeine can increase alertness and can cause insomnia, fine tremors, headache, nervousness, and dizziness. Caffeine has few side effects in most people, but significant side effects can be seen in people with cardiovascular problems (e.g., irregular heartbeat), epilepsy, anxiety, or panic disorder, especially at doses of 300–500 mg. Excess caffeine use is a common contributing cause of insomnia and restlessness. In very large doses (about 10 g), caffeine can cause death, although it is difficult to ingest that amount (a dose of 10 g of caffeine is about the same as drinking 80–110 cups of coffee in a short period of time). There are known cases whereby people consumed very large quantities of caffeine (2–4 g/day) and developed symptoms of mania, paranoid delusions, and hallucinations, which soon abated once they were caffeine-free for several days.

Withdrawal symptoms do occur in people who drink significant amounts of caffeinated beverages every day and then stop. These symptoms include headache, tiredness or fatigue, decreased energy, decreased alertness, drowsiness, sleepiness, decreased well-being, depressed mood, difficulty concentrating, irritability, and feeling foggy-headed. The onset of withdrawal symptoms typically begins 12–24 hr after abstinence, with the peak intensity occurring at 20–51 hr. The duration of withdrawal symptoms ranges from 2 to 9 days.

Caffeine is not considered to be "addicting," in spite of withdrawal symptoms and the development of tolerance (gradually increasing the dose over time to get the same effect). Too often people incorrectly assume that tolerance and withdrawal (which characterizes physical dependence) is also equivalent to "addiction" or chemical dependence. For a drug to be "addicting" (chemical dependence-producing), there must be a unique connection with the receptors in the brain's reward pathway. This has not been shown to occur with caffeine.

Antidepressant Drugs

While these drugs are not classified as CNS stimulants, they do increase mood in depressed individuals and can produce some initial sedation during early use. Their therapeutic use is beyond the scope of this chapter. It is important to note that antidepressants are not dependence-producing ("addictive"), because they have no direct and specific action on the brain's reward pathway. When these drugs are described as "addicting" by the general public, it is because prolonged use can cause withdrawal when people abruptly cease their use. (It is important to remember that withdrawal is *not* the same as addiction.)

These drugs act on portions of the brain's greater limbic system to overcome clinical depression. Drugs in this class range anywhere from tricyclics such as amitriptyline (Elavil) to selective serotonin reuptake inhibitors (SSRIs) such as fluoxetine (Prozac) and escitalopram (Lexapro), as well as serotonin-norepinephrine reuptake inhibitors (SNRI) such as venlafaxine (Effexor). Interestingly, these drugs have replaced benzodiazepines in the treatment of anxiety in the practices of some physicians who are concerned about the chemical dependence produced by benzodiazepines. Antidepressants are not listed in the CSA.

CHAPTER 6

Drugs That Slow Us Down

PATIENTS' OVERVIEW

Opioids such as morphine have been used for centuries to reduce pain and suffering. One of the unique qualities of morphine is that people report, "I still feel the pain but it doesn't bother me." It is this detachment that characterizes the use, abuse, and chemical dependence seen with opioids, in that people feel a dreamy high that is very pleasant. Heroin, one of the world's most abused drugs, although illegal in the United States, is heavily sought after by many, and it is second only to nicotine in its "addictiveness." Heroin dependence is a difficult disease to overcome. Benzodiazepines are notable in their ability to decrease the incidence and severity of anxiety disorders, but they, too, can produce chemical dependence in a percentage of users. In fact, all of the central depressants have dependence liability. Just as the use of barbiturates declined in favor of benzodiazepines, benzodiazepine use in the treatment of anxiety disorders is declining in favor of antidepressant medications.

In certain diseases or conditions, the brain has a tendency to speed up. Particularly in mental states such as pain, anxiety, panic, mania, attention deficit/hyperactivity disorder (ADHD), and epilepsy, it is helpful to have medications to reduce the brain's excessive activity. In ADHD (as discussed in the previous chapter) the state of increased motor activity and inability to focus is best overcome by giving stimulants that increase dopamine function to paradoxically slow the brain. This is because when the normal activity of a part of the frontal lobes that works through dopamine is reduced (in the disease), the "brake" on other parts of the brain is released, and the symptoms of ADHD occur. Stimulants such as the amphetamine Adderall increase dopamine and restore normal function in the affected brain area.

Central nervous system (CNS) depressants have the opposite effects of CNS stimulants and are used primarily to reduce pain, anxiety, panic, mania, and epilepsy. The drugs that reduce pain are called analgesic drugs. Opioids are powerful analgesic drugs, and drugs in the aspirin/ibuprofen category are called anti-inflammatory or "mild" analgesic drugs (these will not be covered because they have little effect on the CNS). The drugs that reduce anxiety and panic are called anxiolytics or (in the old days) minor tranquilizers, and include other sedatives such as doxylamine, the active ingredient in some sleep aids. The drugs that reduce mania include mood stabilizers, antianxiety drugs, some antidepressants, and antipsychotic drugs (antipsychotic drugs will not be covered because they do not produce dependence). Some antidepressants also cause sedation, or sleepiness. The drugs that reduce epilepsy are called antiepileptic drugs (AEDs), antiseizure medications, and sometimes anticonvulsant drugs.

Opioids are known as powerful analgesics and euphoriants, but when abused can cause great harm to the individual (poor health) and to society (illegal trafficking, chemical dependence).

Benzodiazepines are excellent drugs for treating anxiety and enhancing sleep, but when abused can lead to side effects of drowsiness that can affect alertness and driving skills. When used long-term, they can also produce significant withdrawal and chemical dependence in some individuals who use them. Barbiturates are older drugs that have high abuse and dependence liability and, though old, are still around for some isolated therapeutic uses.

Opioids

An opioid is a chemical (naturally occurring in the human body [endogenous] or administered into the body) that binds to opioid receptors in the brain and spinal cord ("central") and in the gastrointestinal tract ("peripheral"). These receptors are involved in the beneficial and side effects of opioids. Although the term *opiate* is often used as a synonym for *opioid*, the term *opioid* includes the natural alkaloids found in the resin of the opium poppy, the semi-synthetic opioids derived from them, and naturally occurring substances called endorphins and enkephalins. The reason for opioid receptors is that the endogenous opioids activate the receptors when mounting responses to pain.

Centrally, the analgesic effects of opioids involve decreased perception of pain, decreased reaction to pain, and increased pain tolerance. The side effects of opioids include sedation, respiratory depression, and constipation. (The phrase "uptight" is Haight-Ashbury era jargon referring to the ability of opiates to cause chronic constipation that becomes a concern to the opioid abuser. Today, "uptight" has become a general statement of feeling stressed.) Opioids are also used for cough suppression and the treatment of diarrhea. Physical dependence (an adaptation of the body to the drugs) can develop with repeated daily administration over a few weeks or long-term administration of opioids, leading to a withdrawal syndrome when the drugs are stopped abruptly. Opioids can produce a feeling of euphoria, and this effect, coupled with physical dependence (mainly tolerance), can lead to recreational use of opioids by some individuals. (Recall that physical dependence is not the same as chemical dependence, or "addiction.")

Common opioids include heroin, morphine, meperidine (Demerol), oxycodone (OxyContin), oxycodone with acetaminophen (Vicodin), methadone, and codeine. These are all "agonist" drugs that stimulate opioid receptors to produce a pharmacological effect. Because of their abuse liability they are placed in Schedule II of the Controlled Substances Act (CSA) (except heroin, which is in Schedule I, and thus is an illegal drug). A drug like buprenorphine (Buprenex, Suboxone) that partially stimulates the receptors is called a "partial agonist." Increasing the dose of this drug produces a plateau effect on the receptors, where increasing the dose past a certain amount will cause no more stimulation of the receptors. Because this drug has lower abuse potential than the full agonist drugs such as morphine, it is placed in Schedule III of the CSA. Finally, drugs such as naloxone and naltrexone, which block the receptors to the effects of an agonist, are called "opioid antagonists." These are not scheduled drugs and are used to treat opioid overdose.

There are three major types of opioid receptors upon which agonists and antagonists can work. These include μ (mu) receptors, which occur in the brain and spinal cord and are mainly involved with producing the effects of euphoria, physical dependence, reduced gastric motility, pinpoint pupils, pain relief, and respiratory depression. The second type are the κ (kappa) receptors, which are involved in sedation, analgesia at the spinal cord level, and pinpoint pupils. The third type are δ (delta) receptors, which occur in the brain and are involved with analgesia, physical dependence, and antidepressant actions. The opioid agonists (drugs that activate opioid receptors) have various effects at different receptors, while naltrexone is an antagonist (opioid receptor blocker) at the μ and κ receptors, and to a lesser extent at the δ receptors.

There are several characteristics of opioids that are unique. First, heroin is an illegal street drug that is a major part of the drug problem in North America. It produces chemical dependence ("addiction") in about 23% of users; therefore, it is *not* true that "if one uses heroin, he/she is an addict." There are a lot of recreational heroin users ("chippers") and abusers who are not dependent and never will be. On the other hand, when the legal drug morphine is prescribed for acute or chronic pain, the incidence of chemical dependence is only about 9%. This suggests that opioid agonists used under control in a therapeutic setting, for pain relief, are a lot less likely to produce chemical dependence ("addiction") than when similar drugs are used on the street. The exact reason for this lower dependence liability is unknown.

Opioids produce perhaps the fastest and largest amount of tolerance of any abused drug. For example, a typical dose to get "high" with heroin would be between 1 and 10 mg. Some experienced users reach a dose of 2 g (2,000 mg) within a month or so, a dose that would kill an inexperienced opioid user. Indeed, opioid tolerance wears off in 2–3 weeks, and if a person goes into treatment, does not use for a while, and then comes out and relapses on the same dose that had been reached before treatment, an overdose will be likely. In addition, opioids produce classic cross-tolerance, in which tolerance developed to one opioid will produce tolerance to other opioids. Thus, when a person is building tolerance to heroin, for example, he is also building tolerance to other opioids. This can be problematic if an experienced heroin user must be treated for a major injury, in which case the normal amount of morphine would have no effect in reducing pain. A similar case arises when a patient is taking naltrexone, an opioid antagonist, for the prevention of relapse to alcohol. If that person must be treated for a major injury, then normal doses of morphine would have no effect in reducing pain. Medical care personnel have to be informed of ongoing medications, so that they will know to increase the morphine dose in a situation such as this. For this reason, naltrexone users can be given wristbands to alert medical personnel of their current medications.

Opioid withdrawal from long-term use (more than 1–2 weeks) can be dramatic and painful. Although death from "cold turkey" opioid withdrawal in otherwise healthy persons does not occur, people often "wish they could die" because of the suffering during withdrawal. Typically starting 6–12 hours after the last dose, the symptoms intensify as the body rebounds from the changed depressed state in an attempt to find a normal level of functioning. In so doing, the body rebounds to a state of hyperexcitability in all nervous systems: the CNS, peripheral nerves, and the autonomic nervous system. Thus there is yawning, runny nose, anxiety, restlessness, insomnia, increased heart rate and blood pressure, extreme sweating accompanied by chills, severe cramping of internal organs and external muscles, diarrhea, nausea, vomiting, and retching (best portrayed in the 1955 movie *The Man with the Golden Arm*). The duration of withdrawal is variable, depending on dose and duration of opioid use, but often lasting 5–10 days (with the most acute effects during the first 2 days). Detoxification (detox) consists of blocking the symptoms with anesthesia (ultra-rapid detox initiated by naltrexone and accompanied by anesthesia or sedation), or by reducing the symptoms with clonidine to treat autonomic symptoms, and sometimes other medications to treat vomiting and diarrhea. Buprenorphine, a partial agonist (partial activator) of the opioid receptors, has been used to reduce the severity of opioid withdrawal in treatment centers, so that patients can participate in opioid dependence treatment earlier. Withdrawal from methadone has an onset that is slower than with heroin and not as severe (controversial) but is more prolonged.

Methadone and buprenorphine are used to treat opioid, and particularly heroin, dependence. These uses are detailed in Chapter 12.

Naloxone (Narcan) is a rapidly acting opioid antagonist that is used in the medication Suboxone. The reason it is mixed into the product containing buprenorphine is to reduce the abuse of the medication by people who are dependent on heroin. When heroin is scarce, some users have turned to the parent medication, Subutex. In these cases the products are crushed and mixed with water before being injected for a "high." The addition of the antagonist naloxone is designed to block the "high" and therefore reduce the abuse. Naloxone is also the injectable medication used to overcome respiratory depression in an opioid user who has overdosed. The speed and selectivity of action of naloxone on opioid overdose is dramatic. Thus, many emergency rooms will use naloxone as an antagonist anytime someone arrives in an emergency room with an unknown overdose, especially if unresponsive with pinpoint pupils. If the person begins breathing again, the overdose was caused by an opioid. If not, no harm has been done and then other measures can be used to overcome the overdose.

Benzodiazepines

Benzodiazepines, typified by diazepam (Valium), were discovered in the 1950s. These medications had become so popular that the Rolling Stones had a hit song in the mid-1960s referring to diazepam as "a little yellow pill" that "gets her through her busy day" in the song "Mother's Little

Helper." Other members of the benzodiazepine class include chlordiazepoxide (Librium), alprazolam (Xanax, one of the most misused drugs), and lorazepam (Ativan). Zolpidem (Ambien) is not structurally a benzodiazepine but its mechanism is equivalent to benzodiazepine-like drugs. Zolpidem is one of the most commonly prescribed sleeping medications for short-term use, and is generally not chemical dependence–producing, although this may change as reports of heavy use accumulate.

Benzodiazepines are psychoactive drugs that increase the effects of the inhibitory neurotransmitter gamma-aminobutyric acid (GABA) in key brain structures, thus causing sedative, hypnotic (sleep-inducing), anxiolytic, anticonvulsant, muscle relaxant, and amnesic actions. The first benzodiazepine, chlordiazepoxide (Librium), was followed three years later by the second most popular benzodiazepine, diazepam (Valium). These drugs are effective in treating anxiety, insomnia, agitation, seizures, muscle spasms, and alcohol withdrawal, and are used as a premedication for surgical or dental procedures. They are classified based upon their duration of action: short, intermediate, or long-acting. Their prescription use is governed by their placement in Schedule IV of the CSA.

Unlike the barbiturates to be described below, benzodiazepines have a greater range of safety and are effective when used therapeutically. Rarely, impairments in thinking, paradoxical aggression, depressed mood, and behavioral impairment (e.g., difficulty in driving) can occur. Generally, these medications are recommended for short-term use, because use longer than 2–3 weeks can lead to tolerance, physical dependence, and perhaps a (mild) withdrawal syndrome. These latter effects are particularly important in the elderly patient, who has reduced kidney and/or liver function and has more difficulty metabolizing these drugs.

Benzodiazepines do not produce a "blockbuster" euphoria, so most abuse and overuse occur in patients prescribed these medications, rather than in the abuse community where extreme "highs" or mellow relaxation is sought. Overdoses with these drugs are rare, unless they are combined with another CNS depressant, such as alcohol.

The treatment for chemical dependence on benzodiazepines is fairly straightforward, but it takes time (weeks) to withdraw from the effects of these drugs. Withdrawal from low to moderate doses is (compared to heroin withdrawal) rather easy, but the hyperexcitability seen in withdrawal from high doses is quite prolonged (3–6 months for chronic long-term withdrawal effects). There are almost never deaths due to withdrawal, and withdrawal severity has been exaggerated by the news media, which erroneously show benzodiazepine withdrawal as being severe. What is not mentioned is that people with dramatic benzodiazepine withdrawal (sometimes culminating in death) are actually withdrawing from multiple depressant drugs.

Benzodiazepines produce a moderate degree of tolerance with long-term use, and there is significant cross-tolerance among the large number of benzodiazepines. There is also what pharmacologists call "cross dependence," which means that any benzodiazepine will substitute for any other benzodiazepine in blocking the signs and symptoms of withdrawal. This fact is useful when an attending physician wishes to substitute a long-acting benzodiazepine for a short-acting benzodiazepine during withdrawal. Such substitution allows the short-acting benzodiazepine patient to undergo a prolonged, rather comfortable withdrawal with a long-acting drug, during which time the dosage is tapered slowly to provide a tolerable withdrawal. Immediate withdrawal from high doses of a benzodiazepine, especially from long-term use, can cause seizures and delirium.

Barbiturates

Is it "bar-BITCH-ur-ate" or "barb-i-TUR-ate"? It's both! Barbiturates are CNS depressant drugs that produce a broad range of effects, from mild sedation to anesthesia. They have been used as hypnotic drugs, antianxiety drugs, antiepileptics, and as adjuncts to full general anesthesia. They produce chemical dependence, and are highly abused when freely available. In addition, they have the potential for lethal overdose, especially when mixed with other depressants such as alcohol. This is why their use is now restricted and as a drug class they have mostly been replaced with the benzodiazepines for the treatment of anxiety and insomnia. However, the drugs are still available for use in anesthesia, epilepsy, and occasionally for the treatment of insomnia. Drugs in this class include pentobarbital and secobarbital (for sleep, Schedule II), thiopental (induction to anesthesia, Schedule III), and phenobarbital (epilepsy treatment, Schedule IV).

Barbiturates are described according to their onset and duration of action. Ultrashort-acting barbiturates (e.g., thiopental, Pentothal) produce unconsciousness within seconds of intravenous injection and are used to prepare patients for surgery; then other longer-acting agents can be given to maintain a surgical plane of anesthesia. Their abuse potential is low because they are typically used in hospital settings and are not used orally. (Sodium Pentothal is also known as "truth serum," which is an erroneous name. However, when people lose their inhibitions under this drug, they are less likely to be aware of what they should or should not say!)

Pentobarbital and secobarbital are intermediate-acting barbiturates used for sleep. Their onset is about 20–30 min after oral administration and their duration is typically 4–6 hr. The long-acting barbiturates such as phenobarbital have a longer onset (1–2 hr) but long duration (around 12 hr) and are used in the treatment of epilepsy. In the past, phenobarbital was used to treat insomnia and anxiety. In spite of its low abuse potential, it has been replaced for these uses by the benzodiazepines; however, it is an important option in treating seizures in veterinary care.

Barbiturates exert their action on the brain through an enhancement of the effects of GABA, an inhibitory neurotransmitter. Briefly, when a drug increases GABA function in certain brain areas, those brain areas will be less stimulated and will slow down. This is particularly effective in treating epilepsy, in which brain cells are rapidly firing for various known and unknown reasons.

CHAPTER 7

Drug Use and Abuse in Adolescents

with Mark Evan Goldman, PhD

PATIENTS' OVERVIEW

Drug problems in adolescents constitute one of the most difficult problems in this field. Not only are adolescents extremely susceptible to drug use and abuse (because of availability and peer acceptance), but the effects of drugs on this population are much greater than in adults. There appears to be an enhanced vulnerability to chemical dependence, drugs seem to have greater toxicity in adolescents, and risk-taking behavior in adolescents causes the use of greater quantities and newer drugs that pharmacologists know little about. Finally, drug prevention programs seem to have little effect in this population because of immature decision-making areas of the adolescent brain.

Adolescence can be defined as a transitory period of time in human development characterized by a variety of physiologic, psychological, and social changes. Typical age ranges for adolescence are 10–18 or 13–24, and will vary based upon culture and literature source. There is dichotomous evidence that the age of first "experimenting" with drugs is earlier or later than "traditional" adolescence. For example, these days young people are "trying" alcohol and other drugs at earlier ages than in the past. In contrast, some clinicians believe that a delay by many adolescents in experimenting with abusable drugs is due to the constant presence of parental figures, coaches, and demanding activities during the high school years. Then, upon graduating and being in the presence of peers in college, in the military, or in the workplace, the micromanagement is reduced and the "older adolescent" (young adult) then needs to make personal choices for the first time. For whatever reason, those choices may fall on the side of "trying" drugs.

Because adolescents have potential access to the same drugs and prescriptions as adults, the realm of usable and abusable drugs in adolescents includes the same categories as in the adult population. One major difference between adults and adolescents, however, is the motivating factor to "experiment" or to start using and abusing chemicals, especially when in the presence of peers. For example, sorority and fraternity parties are common places to binge, sometimes to the point of unconsciousness or cessation of breathing. Also, today adolescents tend to favor celebrity and sports role models to define their lifestyles. The behaviors of celebrity superstars such as Lindsay Lohan and Miley Cyrus (as extreme role models) seem to define the actions of adolescents.

Owners of major sports franchises including the National Football League (NFL), Major League Baseball (MLB), and National Basketball Association (NBA) have been increasingly vocal when their players exhibit poor judgment "off the field" because they are role models for children. These lapses in judgment by professionals have included the abuse of steroidal performance-enhancing drugs, acute and chronic drug abuse, and abusive personality traits such as domestic partner abuses. Similarly, "Joe Kool" advertisements and the use of flavored tobaccos have strongly influenced adolescents by implying that tobacco use is a positive behavior. The use of tobacco products occurs in spite of years of educational training in schools and, sometimes, houses of worship, describing the acute and chronic harm of drug abuse. Might this drug use in spite of training occur because of a difference in the physiology of adolescents?

Adolescent Physiology

There is scientific evidence that the adolescent human body is insufficiently developed to handle drug abuse. First, the liver and renal system (kidneys) have not yet completely matured to be able to metabolize medications or drugs as rapidly as the liver and kidneys in adults. For example, some adolescents have a smaller body size than adults, so a smaller drug or medication dose may be required for efficacy and reduced toxicity.

Perhaps more important, new brain-imaging evidence indicates that the frontal lobes of the brain do not fully mature until the age of about 21–24 years. This is of major importance when we realize that the frontal lobes are the "executive function" part of the brain. These are the areas where decision making, judgment, and impulse control occur. So if these are underfunctioning in adolescents, what happens? Obviously, the adolescent is less able to make appropriate decisions or proper judgments, and impulses prevail. So even after a drug prevention program, an adolescent may understand the importance of not using drugs (and can even pass a test on the material), but when the real-world situation of making a choice between using and not using presents itself, the wrong choice is often made. So far, there is no known way to "hurry" the maturation of the frontal lobes, but there is some evidence that parental guidance, more education, choice-making exercises, and even more guidance in making choices in early life might be helpful.

Unfortunately, the human use of drugs early in life appears to slow maturation of the frontal lobes, and even to block further maturation of the brain and subsequent emotional maturity in heavy drinkers and drug users.

The Gateway Drug Theory

Historically, scientists, sociologists, and clinicians have proposed that the use of three "soft" drugs of abuse (alcohol, marijuana, and tobacco) lead to subsequent abuse of stronger substances ("hard drugs") and possibly to an increased potential for committing crime. Inherent in the nature of scientists, sociologists, and clinicians is the desire to define concepts by calling a pattern a "hypothesis" or, even worse, a "theory," in this case, the "gateway drug theory." As a result of labeling something as a hypothesis or theory, others will oppose such labeling and find reasons to find fault with the premise. (For example, there is no evidence to show that the early use of alcohol, marijuana, or tobacco *causes* the use of harder drugs; the simple availability of legal drugs might cause them to be used earlier.) It is difficult to come to a conclusion on this issue, because cause and effect are always hard to pin down in science. On the one hand, there are many studies showing a correlation between the use of alcohol, tobacco, or cannabis and the later use of hard drugs (cocaine, opiates, hallucinogenic mushrooms, and synthetic hallucinogens). It is a fact that most people under the age of 21 have easy access to alcohol, tobacco, and marijuana. It is logical, therefore, that alcohol, tobacco, and marijuana would be abused prior to other substances. For example, a 10-year study of almost 2,000 Australians concluded that adult amphetamine users were more likely to have abused other drugs at earlier ages

(Degenhardt et al., 2007). On the other hand, a Virginia study concluded that both cannabis *and* genetic influences contribute to the use of other drugs. Given all the available evidence to date, the gateway drug theory has still not been proven.

Adolescent Alcohol Use

Clearly, alcohol is the most abused substance in people under the age of 21 around the world. In the United States, alcohol-related injuries and deaths decreased substantially when the legal drinking age was raised from 18 to 21. In the United Kingdom, binge drinking and alcohol-related antisocial behaviors are increasing, suggesting that the UK should adopt the 21-and-over law as well as increase taxation on alcohol beverages, to more closely mirror the benefits of these policies in the United States.

Binge drinking is defined in the United States as a pattern of drinking alcohol that brings blood alcohol concentration (BAC) to 0.08% or above. For the typical adult, this pattern corresponds to consuming five or more drinks (male), or four or more drinks (female), in about two hours.

In addition to adolescent alcohol use leading to additional drug use, there is ample evidence that adolescent alcohol use more readily leads to adult alcohol abuse and dependence. For example, early epidemiological studies have found that adolescents who begin drinking at age 14 have an estimated lifetime prevalence risk for alcohol dependence of 47%. Conversely, adolescents who begin drinking alcohol at age 20 have about one-fourth the estimated lifetime prevalence risk (Grant & Dawson, 1997). This says that the brain's reward pathway (where alcohol dependence occurs) can be dysregulated earlier and more strongly by early drug use. This may be because the immature brain reward pathway is further slowed in its development by alcohol (and perhaps by other drugs). Several more recent studies have confirmed this phenomenon of early drinking causing more alcohol dependence.

Education programs for preadults and their families stress abstinence. Abstinence is refraining from the use of alcoholic beverages, and this behavior implies "willful avoidance" and, therefore, self-control. (However, not all drinking can be controlled, as described in Chapters 1 and 18.)

Adolescent Tobacco Use

Tobacco possesses the same toxicity in adolescents as in adults. Because adolescents are likely to live longer than people who are significantly older, the long-term health consequences of tobacco use in adolescents are magnified. Also, adolescents tend to have fewer resources (financial and treatment options) to get successful treatment for nicotine dependence. Thus, the American Academy of Pediatrics supports the U.S. Public Health Guidelines of the "5 As": Ask, Advise, Assess, Assist, and Arrange, in helping adolescents stop smoking.

For all of the reasons listed above, adolescents are less likely to volunteer tobacco consumption issues to medical professionals. As a result, health care providers are urged to observe each adolescent for signs of chronic tobacco use, including such indications as the tobacco smell, yellowing teeth, and reduced pulmonary function.

Treatment of many medical health diseases is relatively straightforward, for example, a bacterial infection can be accurately pinpointed, thus opening a spectrum of obvious choices to the medical team. Team members, such as pharmacists and nurses, can identify potential iatrogenic (drug-induced) effects such as prior allergic responses. Treatment of the adolescent tobacco addict, however, is highly dependent upon a plan that the treatment specialist and adolescent can agree upon.

Unlike with adults, nicotine replacement therapy (NRT) in adolescents is complicated by state laws and regulations. In some states, for example, medications must be dispensed by on-site personnel such as school nurses. With the number of school nurses being curtailed by fiscal budgets, the availability of on-site dispensers of midday NRT is reduced. This reality needs to be addressed by the treatment team and may sway the team into using treatments that do not necessitate a midday dose.

Cannabis (Marijuana)

For several decades, the National Institute on Drug Abuse (NIDA) has monitored drug use patterns in U.S. adolescent populations. In the 1970s, cannabis use among high school students peaked, with as many as 70% of students "using" cannabis regularly. More recently, cannabis use has leveled off in high school students (SAMHSA, 2009).

As with smoking tobacco, the inhalation of crude cannabis plant material is toxic and includes the inhalation of carcinogens. Because the acute inhalation of cannabis is "deeper" than tobacco, there is an increased risk for more toxins to be inhaled per puff than with tobacco. Starting at an adolescent age, cumulative cannabis use of more than 8 years has been shown to have major negative effects on pulmonary function. In addition, adolescent cannabis users have an increased risk of depression, suicide, psychosis, unprotected sex, and delinquent behavior, including school dropout and running away from home.

Similarly, studies have demonstrated that in places where there is easy access to cannabis, cannabis is the drug that is abused first. In California, there is an active debate about legalizing cannabis and taxing its production and sale. While this state's process is perceived to be income generation (taxation), there is ongoing debate about enforcement to minimize the impact on people under the age of legal use.

Some factors may minimize cannabis use in adolescents. These factors include routine eating of dinner meals as a family unit (including regular active positive family conversations), allowing family to meet friends, and giving opinions about potential friends that might have a bad social influence on adolescents and their participation in "after-the-bell" school activities.

There are many factors that affect risk potential for initial adolescent cannabis use. Among the negative risk factors are: comorbid factors (attention deficit/hyperactivity disorder [ADHD], conduct disorders [CDs], antisocial personality disorder [APD]), family factors (abuse of substances by family members, chaotic home issues, abusive family members), environment (easy access, peers who are users), and school associations (low academic standards, lack of involvement in required school activities). For each of the negative risk factors listed above, a simple dialogue between clinician and adolescent can lead to ideas to replace the negative associations with ones that will minimize the likelihood of future bad choices by the adolescent.

Prescription Drug Abuse

This topic includes any use of a Schedule II–Schedule V drug outside the prescription written by the legal (U.S. Food and Drug Administration [FDA]–approved) health care provider. This includes use by anyone except the patient on the prescription, taking too much of the drug or taking the drug more frequently than prescribed, donating the drug to another person, or selling the drug to another person. In other words, any diversion of the medication is prescription drug abuse. By definition, this topic is limited to medications; however, California and other states allow (will allow) medical personnel to write prescriptions for cannabis, so it is likely that cannabis will also become a prescription drug of abuse.

In many cases, adolescents have easy access to prescription medications, including prescription drugs that are obtained from family members, drugs procured from prescription "pads" that are stolen then forged, and prescription drugs that are legally obtained and then sold. Major medications that are abused include amphetamines, opioids, and benzodiazepines.

Steroid Abuse

Anabolic performance-enhancing steroid abuse, according to some sources, is rampant among adolescent athletes and bodybuilders. Anabolic steroids not only produce a mild euphoria, they have side effects of increasing muscle mass and strength. Thus it is not surprising that young people involved in football, baseball, wrestling, and track would find these drugs attractive. To some young athletes, using such drugs is considered necessary to become and remain competitive in situations where becoming a professional athlete is a possibility. Even some athletes in sports such as tennis, golf, and cheerleading have used performance-enhancing steroids. The problem with steroid abuse is more about drug toxicity than chemical dependence. The development of steroid dependence has not yet been proven.

Club Drugs

The traditional club drugs, named by the National Institute on Drug Abuse on its website (2010) are MDMA (methylenedioxymethamphetamine, or ecstasy), LSD (lysergic acid diethylamide, or just "acid"), methamphetamine (or meth), ketamine (special K, vitamin K), GHB (gamma-hydroxybutyrate, liquid ecstasy), and Rohypnol (roofies). These drugs are often used in clubs or "raves"—large get-togethers, mostly of young people, where disc jockeys and synchronized light shows are featured, and where drug use is allowed (along with alcohol). Club-drug users agree that the drugs enhance the club environment, which unfortunately often leads young people to overuse and sometimes overdose. Particularly in combination with alcohol, these drugs are highly dangerous in young people, who are often preoccupied and not thinking about the dangerous combinations they are consuming, and dancing in a crowded space (increasing the potential for dehydration and elevated body temperature).

Methamphetamine was discussed in Chapter 5 as a member of the amphetamine family. Ecstasy is chemically related to amphetamines but has a different effect on the neurochemistry of the brain. Unlike amphetamines, it produces a dreamy high, and users at raves often take it to enhance the music and to increase energy. LSD is an older drug, less popular than it was 50 years ago, but still common enough that adolescents have easy access to it. LSD is the prototypical hallucinogenic drug, and highly potent; only a few micrograms are needed to produce an effect, whereas most "pill" form drugs require several milligrams—1,000 times more—to be effective. There is no known lethal dose of LSD in humans; however, people on an LSD "trip" can die, when visual hallucinations and delusions cause the person, for example, to think he or she can fly.

Ketamine, formerly a human surgical anesthetic, has a number of side effects in humans that are not found in animals. Thus it is commonly used for animal surgery anesthesia, which makes it available as a street drug (via diversion or theft from veterinary offices). Ketamine, along with its street companion phencyclidine (known as PCP or angel dust) produces a distorted view of the world along with a feeling of light anesthesia. It is more dangerous than LSD; users at rave parties can develop high blood pressure, catatonia (inability to move), and coma.

GHB, formerly used by body builders to help decrease body fat and increase muscle mass (now outlawed), is available by prescription (Xyrem) for the treatment of cataplexy associated with narcolepsy (in which people fall asleep at inappropriate times). Street GHB is very potent and very toxic, and overdoses can occur easily.

Rohypnol is an illegal (in the United States) benzodiazepine that has all the characteristics of this drug class as described in Chapter 6; it reduces anxiety, promotes sleep, and causes a dreamy sedation. It is the prototypical "date rape drug" in which a cocktail of rohypnol and alcohol can cause deep sedation and amnesia, leading to date rapes in which the victim is incapacitated and often has no memory of what happened.

The dependence potential of this class of drugs is variable. Methamphetamine dependence is probably the highest of the club drugs (estimated at something over 10% of users), with rohypnol dependence probably in the range of 9%, LSD at about 5%, and the others unknown (Table 1.1).

Inhalants

This class of chemicals—which includes gasoline, Freon, toluene, nitrites, and nitrous oxide—is used commercially in fuels, medicinals, and products such as airplane glue, paint remover, model toy paints, and refrigerants. Teenagers and adolescents often use these products (which are often less expensive and more easily available than alcohol) to get a high, without knowing that they are extremely dangerous to body organs. They have very high toxicity when inhaled (through a process known as "huffing"), and can cause cardiac arrhythmia or stoppage (heart attack) and respiratory freezing (such as with Freon), leading to almost instant cessation of breathing and blood flow. A large number of first-time users die of overdose with inhalants.

Abused Over-the-Counter Drugs

Over-the-counter (OTC) drugs could more correctly be called "off the shelf" drugs. Most OTC items are stocked on shelves and do not require a prescription. One major OTC class is cough/cold medications that contain more than one ingredient: doxylamine (a sedating antihistamine found in products such as NyQuil), alcohol (up to 10 %), as well as dextromethorphan (DMX, cough suppressant, also found in Robitussin, an abused cough medicine). "Cold and flu" versions of these products may also contain acetaminophen (an analgesic or painkiller) and phenylephrine (a decongestant). Operators of clandestine laboratories have used OTC medications, especially phenylephrine, as ingredients for the synthesis of methamphetamine.

Diphenhydramine is an oral OTC antihistamine that is used to aid sleep. One common trade name for this drug is Benadryl™, and some teenagers like this medicine for the sedation it produces. Other OTC drug abuse involves laxatives and emetics (e.g., Emetrol) as weight-loss tools. The non-medical use of these products to lose weight can be dangerous, since these can cause dehydration and electrolyte loss.

CHAPTER 8

Visual and Behavioral Signs of Drug Abuse

PATIENTS' OVERVIEW

Parents, teachers, and law enforcement personnel are always interested in signs of drug use in children and adolescents. Even in adults it is important to detect the first signs of drug use so that problems do not escalate. Employers should be aware of such signs, for drug use will often reduce work efficiency. This chapter lists the signs of drug use in the drugs that might be found in the workplace, in the schoolroom, or at home.

There are many visual and behavioral signs of drug use and misuse. In this chapter, general signs of drug use and misuse are discussed, followed by a drug-by-drug listing, including specific visual and behavioral signs associated with each drug. This is not a science, however, and thus signs such as a runny nose can mean either cocaine snorting or a cold or allergy. Thus it is important that the observer determine that several signs are occurring that helps to pin down drug use. Of course, there is nothing more incriminating than finding marijuana joints in a sock drawer!

General Behavioral Signs and Symptoms of Drug Use

Drug use in individuals begins with casual use or social use of the drug in groups. As the individual continues to "use" (because the drug produces a good feeling), often more and more of the drug is needed because of the buildup of tolerance. In a person who is genetically vulnerable to chemical dependence, a compulsion to take the drug becomes more apparent, the person uses on a daily basis, and the barriers set up to keep family and friends from finding out about the drug use begin to go down. Unfortunately, by the time that apparent symptoms of drug use are seen, the individual is already a heavy drug user.

It is important to watch for *changes* in behavior, attitudes, personality, or appearance. However, some of these symptoms might also be caused by stress, changes in schools as parents move, or even poor parenting skills. A mental health professional should be contacted if several of these symptoms persist without explanation.

Signs (what the observer sees) and symptoms (what the user feels) that might suggest drug use:

- The presence of drug paraphernalia, such as syringes, glass tubes, and pipes
- A change in friends, particularly with some degree of secrecy about what they do together
- A sudden avoidance of an old crowd, change in activities or hobbies
- A drop in grades or job performance or attendance at school or work
- Acting silly or giddy
- Secretive or suspicious behavior, demanding more privacy, locking doors
- A change in personal grooming habits
- Mood swings, nervousness, irritability, paranoia, depression
- A sudden increase in sensitivity, tantrums, or aggressiveness
- A change in mood, motivation, self-esteem, energy, or appetite
- A reduction in attentiveness; forgetfulness, blackouts
- A change in attitude about doing things with the family
- Being more prone to accidents, argumentative, more combative
- Having an unexplained need for money; theft, stealing, illegal activity
- The disappearance of things of value around the house; missing prescriptions
- Telling lies, evading questions, becoming silent, avoiding eye contact
- An increase in risky behavior, such as unprotected sex, car racing, staying out late

- A new interest in clothes, music, other items related to drug use
- Using incense, perfume, mouthwash, or air freshener to mask the smell of drugs or smoke
- Talking about or texting "420" (pronounced four-twenty, not four-hundred-twenty), a code for smoking marijuana

General Physical Signs of Drug Use

Physical signs are the result of the drug's action on the body or the administration of drugs. Here are some that apply to the use of many drugs:

- Change in appetite, eating habits, or sudden weight loss or gain
- Sleep disruption, signs of sleepiness during the day
- Extreme hyperactivity or excessive talking, or being withdrawn or sullen
- Complaints of irregular heartbeat or "scary" heart racing
- Nausea, vomiting, diarrhea, sweating
- Runny nose, persistent cough
- Needle "tracks" on arms, legs, neck, between toes, even on the back of the hands
- Fine tremors of the hands, feet, head
- Red, bloodshot, watery eyes, unusual pupil size, blank stare
- Blushing or pale cheeks
- Unsteady on feet, poor coordination, slurred speech
- Unusual smells on the breath, body, or clothing

Signs of Specific Drug Use

Signs of use can vary significantly from one drug to another.

Marijuana (pot, reefer, grass, weed, dope, ganja, mary jane, hash)
There is an excellent discussion of marijuana use and myths on the Web site www.theantidrug.com. In general, the use of marijuana produces the following effects:

- Bloodshot eyes
- Blank or dazed stare
- Sleeping late
- Illogical talking, slurred speech
- Suddenly being very hungry
- Inappropriate laughing
- Sweet burnt scent on the body
- Loss of motivation
- Short-term memory loss
- Weight gain or loss
- Anxiety or paranoia

Alcohol (booze)

Anyone who has consumed more than one serving of alcohol can recognize these features:

- Persistent odor of alcohol, not due to (the short-acting smell of) mouthwash
- Slurred speech
- Poor judgment
- Difficulty walking
- Delayed reaction to stimuli
- Clumsiness; bumping into other people, tables, walls
- Sleepiness
- Inappropriate or loud talking
- Being passed out
- (Sometimes) aggressiveness; (other times) being lonely, apologetic, withdrawn

Tobacco/Nicotine (fags, cigs, smoke)

- Smell of smoke, tobacco
- Stained fingers or teeth
- Persistent cough
- Restlessness, irritability (nicotine withdrawal)
- Spitting
- Depression, anxiety, possible suicidal behavior

Stimulants (cocaine, amphetamines)—cocaine (coke, snow, nose candy, blow, Big C, powder, crack, rock, freebase, cookie), amphetamines (speed, uppers, black beauties, hearts), methamphetamine (crank, crystal meth, speed)

- Hyperactivity, excessive talking
- Feeling "high," illogical talking
- Irritability, grouchiness, agitation
- Anxiety (with high doses), followed by depression
- Increased energy, long periods of time without sleeping
- Sleeps late after no sleep
- Altered sleep/wake cycles
- Dilated pupils
- Reduced appetite, weight loss
- Dry mouth, sweating
- Decreased sex drive
- Runny nose, sniffing (cocaine by inhalation)
- Erratic behavior (methamphetamine)

- "Meth mouth"—broken, stained teeth (methamphetamine)
- Scabs on arms, face, legs (methamphetamine)

Depressants (benzodiazepine sedatives and barbiturates)—barbiturates (downers, barbs, blue devils, red devils, yellows), benzodiazepines (trade names used: Valium, Librium, Serax)

- Signs of drunkenness but without the smell of alcohol
- Clumsiness, slurred speech
- Difficulty concentrating
- Disorientation
- Relaxed muscles
- Poor judgment
- Sleepiness, laziness

Opioids (including heroin)—heroin (smack, horse, mud, junk, black tar, Big H)

- Needle marks (especially with heroin)
- Poor hygiene (especially with heroin)
- Sleepiness, or (with heroin) "nodding," a dreamlike state, near sleep, for minutes or hours
- Sweating, vomiting, muscle cramps, shivering, skin-crawling sensations (signs of withdrawal)
- Pinpoint pupils, unresponsive to light
- Loss of appetite
- Twitching

Hallucinogens (LSD, mescaline, psilocybin)—acid, magic mushrooms, "shrooms," buttons, cactus

- Dilated pupils
- False sense of power
- Distortion of time and space
- Hallucinations
- Delusional thinking
- Misperceptions—perceiving people or objects as something else
- Bizarre and irrational behavior, including aggression, mood swings
- Loss of control, anxiety, panic
- Increased ego
- Confusion
- Helplessness

Inhalants (gasoline, toluene, paint thinner, aerosols, airplane glue, nitrites)

- Watery eyes
- Giggling, silliness, dizziness
- Impaired vision
- Impaired thought and memory
- Impairment of reasoning
- Headaches and nausea
- Fainting ("going unconscious")
- Anxiety
- Irritability
- Poor coordination
- Loss of hearing or sense of smell
- Difficulty breathing
- Cardiac arrest
- Irreversible brain damage

How to Tell If You Have a Drug Abuse Problem

Some people who use drugs sometimes wonder whether they have a drug problem. Here is a series of questions that can be used by anyone who can be honest about the answers (adapted from HelpGuide.org, 2010).

- Do you feel as if you can't stop, even if you wanted to?
- Do you ever feel bad or guilty about your alcohol or other drug use?
- Do you need to use alcohol or drugs to relax or feel better?
- Do your friends or family members complain or worry about your alcohol or other drug use?
- Do you hide your alcohol or other drug use or lie about it?
- Have you ever done anything illegal in order to obtain alcohol or other drugs?
- Do you spend money on alcohol or other drugs that you really can't afford?
- Do you ever use more than one recreational drug at a time?
- Have you ever failed a field sobriety test or had a positive urine screen?

If you answered yes to one or more of the questions, you may or do have a drug problem. Talk to a clinician (such as a drug counselor) for advice.

CHAPTER 9

Gender and Cultural Differences in Drug Use

with Mark Evan Goldman, PhD

PATIENTS' OVERVIEW

Because past drug studies often did not include both genders, today there is a great interest in comparing drug effects in men and women. Also, there are many anecdotal beliefs about the vulnerability of certain cultures to drugs (e.g., the belief that Irish are heavily alcoholic). Thus research has been increasing in this area, and some interesting findings are now available. Anyone interested in "addiction" will find this information valuable in helping overcome some old, mistaken beliefs.

Generally, men are more likely to use and abuse drugs than women, but women are more vulnerable to the effects of drugs. While this suggests that women might be more likely to become chemically dependent, statistics say otherwise. For example, there are 3 times as many male alcoholics as women alcoholics. The reasons for this are not clear. Hormones might contribute to this vulnerability, but genes do not seem to be involved. Alcohol dependence is not gender-linked, according to the latest studies. So what are the gender differences in alcohol and other drug use, abuse, and dependence? And what causes them? The answers are not totally clear, but there have been some interesting studies.

Gender Differences in Response to Alcohol

It is true that the earliest studies in the science of alcohol and alcoholism were mostly carried out in males—both human and animal. Men and male rats and mice were used primarily because of their lesser variability due to sex hormone fluctuations. In animal studies, male animals were generally larger and easier to use for brain chemistry studies. Likewise, alcoholic men were easier to find and their greater numbers lent themselves to larger studies. It was the larger numbers of studies on males that prompted the National Institutes of Health (NIH) in the 1980s to strongly encourage, and then urge, the inclusion of women and minorities in all health-related research in the United States. This culminated, after some political wrangling, in the NIH Revitalization Act of 1993, which mandated the inclusion of women and minorities in clinical research. Although this act was directed at increasing research in women and minorities, it had a strong trickle-down effect in increasing basic animal research that included both genders.

Today, research on women's health has expanded greatly. While it's true that men are more likely to drink alcohol and in greater quantities, women are more likely to develop problems (and earlier than men) from drinking alcohol. This begins with the fact that each alcoholic drink in a woman produces a higher blood alcohol concentration (BAC), compared with the same drink in a man. Thus, women develop alcohol-induced levels of damage at lower levels of drinking over a shorter period of time. This means that, in general, women are at higher risk for liver disease, heart disease, and other diseases associated with alcohol consumption (Greenfield et al., 2010).

Because of high BACs, the fetus is at great risk for a fetal alcohol spectrum disorder (FASD), including the devastating fetal alcohol syndrome (FAS). However, even relatively low doses of alcohol (one to two drinks) can cause fetal alcohol effects (FAE). Women who drink have a slightly elevated risk for breast cancer, and there may be differences between drinking men and women in the incidence of heart disease, osteoporosis, memory and brain function, and interactions between alcohol and medications, particularly in the elderly. More research is needed to sort out the real differences.

Finally, results from national surveys (e.g., SAMHSA, 2009) show that alcohol use occurs frequently in both adolescents and young adults, and the number of young women who drink heavily is quite high. This means that adolescent female-related concerns might be enhanced; emotional difficulties, depression, problems with self-image, risk-taking behaviors, and perceived stress could all be exacerbated by the drinking of alcohol.

Gender Differences in Response to Tobacco

Around 71 million Americans ages 12 and older said they smoked cigarettes in 2008, and around 35% of men and 23% of women said they smoked tobacco at that time (Harvard Mental Health Letter, 2010). We know that female smokers are more vulnerable to certain health risks than male smokers. They are more likely to develop lung cancer and are twice as likely to have a heart attack. In addition, women find it more difficult to quit smoking than men and are more likely to restart smoking after they quit. It may be that women are more responsive to environmental cues and triggers (such as cigarette advertising, or wanting to smoke while drinking alcohol).

Women do start smoking cigarettes at an earlier age than men. The fastest-growing segment of new smokers in the U.S. population is adolescent girls. On the other end of the smoking cycle, adolescent girls and women are often afraid of weight gain when they stop smoking, and this may slow the smoking cessation process. Obviously weight gain does not occur in all people who stop smoking, and it might be productive to help women learn to accept any weight gain as reasonable and a trade-off for their smoke-free improved health.

Gender differences in response to other drugs of abuse are sadly lacking. More research is urgently needed on differences between men and women using marijuana, opioids, stimulants (including amphetamines and cocaine), and street drugs such as LSD, ecstasy, ketamine, and GHB. More research is also needed in the areas of dependence liability, withdrawal severity, and abuse vulnerability to all drugs in terms of gender differences.

Gender Differences in Vulnerability to Drug Abuse and Dependence

Recent epidemiologic studies indicate that men are 2.2 times more likely than women to abuse drugs (especially daily marijuana), and 1.9 times more likely to have chemical dependence (Greenfield et al., 2010). Data on prescription drugs are less consistent.

Telescoping is a term used to describe an accelerated progression from the first use of a drug to the onset of dependence and first-time treatment (Greenfield et al., 2010). Studies typically report telescoping in women for opioids, cannabis, and alcohol. Thus, upon first admission to treatment, women seem to have a more severe clinical profile than men, even though men may have used more of the substance for a longer period of time than women.

Causes of Cultural Differences in Drug Use and the Response to Drugs

Genetics research helps describe "what we are" based upon our genetic blueprints, that is, our genotype. Knowledge of our genotype can be quantified by "sequencing" our genes, especially those alleles (gene variants) that could put us at risk for diseases. Such differences are already measurable; numerous tests are available to estimate a person's risks for genetic diseases ranging from Alzheimer's disease to breast cancer. Medical professionals such as clinical geneticists can order specialized tests to determine the risk of rare diseases such as cystic fibrosis and Tay-Sachs disease. In addition to "orders" from a medical professional, there are now consumer "over-the-counter" test kits that can be utilized by anyone to achieve some of these results. (However, media reports have recently questioned the accuracy of over-the-counter test kits.)

Then there is the phenotype (clinical characteristic), which can give observers a view of our background through our appearance, speech pattern, or physical features. Often, by talking with people or knowing their background, we can learn how they are influenced by their prior and current surroundings, that is, their cultural heritage or, simply, their culture. Just within the United States, there are at least seven obvious cultures, including Caucasians, African Americans, Hispanics, Pacific Islanders, Native Americans, Middle Easterners, and Alaskan Americans. Of course, these categories can be further subdivided.

Similarly, by understanding the quantitative aspects of race, we may have a better understanding of ways to teach and inform members of those groups, in effect a "personalized medicine" (i.e., a "personal genomic history"). Thus, we may be able to tailor a personal pharmaceutical plan. This process is actually done for many patients with specific diseases, for example, a doctor does not prescribe an antibiotic until the "sensitivity" of the infectious agent to the antibiotic is known.

There are many ways to examine our cultures that may give an estimate of our preferences, especially with respect to drug use. For example, we could quickly list global regions and their alcohol beverage preferences: Mexico (beer, tequila), United Kingdom (beer, Scotch), United States (beer, wines), and Europe (wines, whiskey). But the differences could be much more tightly defined, such as across the border between Israel and Palestine—blocks apart, yet different cultural worlds where alcohol can or cannot be used. Or Miami and Havana, which are just 70 miles of ocean away from each other; they are very culturally similar due to families on each side of the border, yet one side enjoys more democratic freedoms than the other.

From the other view, cultural influences in the form of "cultural pride" are increasingly acting as a deterrent to drug abuse by teaching each group that they should not succumb to their cultural backgrounds. These efforts are manifest in "house of worship" participation by various cultural groups. In New York City, for example, there is an annual Puerto Rican Pride parade where estimates suggest that there are more self-proclaimed Puerto Ricans in attendance than there are people on the entire island of Puerto Rico. Similarly, Cinqo de Mayo is a huge celebration across the southwestern United States that is enjoyed by people of many cultures. If the fifth day of May does not fall on a weekend, some establishments advertise that Cinqo de Mayo will be held on the closest weekend day, in addition to the actual day it is named after. Another example is that many people become temporarily "Irish" on Saint Patrick's Day. All of these celebrations, of course, involve the use and abuse of alcohol and other drugs.

In the South Pacific islands, including Hawaii, a cultural activity is consumption of a water-extracted root from the plant called *Piper methysticum*. The general name of the beverage is simply kava. Like hookah (water pipe for smoking) and tobacco lounges, many "kava bars" sell the beverage as part of a group experience, typically in the evening. According to a review of the literature, the crude cold-water extract from the root does have efficacy in humans as an antianxiety treatment. This plant is rich in kavalactones, although controlled studies have not decoded its exact mechanism. In addition, the consumer is not always clear about whether the beverage comes from the true kava root or a mistaken plant or plant part with no kavalactones. Material from the plant may also be toxic to the liver.

Cultural Access to Psychedelic Plant-Derived Material

Historically, materials from psychedelic plants have been used in religious practices over the millennia. Even in the Judeo-Christian religions, drug use has been described. For example, ancient Jews were anointed with holy oils extracted from cannabis.

Western scientists (e.g., R. E. Schultes, Harvard University) have conducted numerous scientific studies of active psychoactive plants. Prior to his death, Schultes was a frequent visitor to the Amazon, where he conducted ethnobotanical (ethnic practices and use of plants) studies (e.g.,

Shultes & Hofmann, 1979). These often involved firsthand experience of the ceremonies, including participation in the consumption of the plant-derived materials, and then (if possible) writing about the experience in scientific journals.

Besides the Amazon, scientists have also turned to understanding Eastern medicines that have been used as therapies for many centuries. Pharmaceutical companies have attempted both to understand the "science" behind the culture and to capitalize on potential Western-like drugs that could be manufactured and sold as ethical pharmaceutical medications.

Psychoactive parts of a plant may include the bark, bean, stem, root, leaf, bud or (rarely) fruit. A short list of naturally derived psychoactive substances includes tryptamines such as dimethyl tryptamine (DMT) and its methoxy derivatives, tetrahydrocannabinol, alkaloids, β (beta)-carbolines, mescaline from some mushrooms, tetrahydroharman, numerous phenethylamines and naturally occurring amphetamines. A practice among "educated" psychedelic plant users is to place one sample of the material being used in a refrigerator. In case of a medical emergency, the first responders will check the refrigerator to see if the sample of the toxic material can be used to help identify the cause of the symptoms and, thus, a potential treatment.

Nicotine and cocaine are mood-altering, but they are not as typically used in religious practices (except for Native Americans who use tobacco in ceremonial use) as are substances such as hallucinogens. Culturally, however, smoking flavored tobacco is often used in hookah lounges in traditional cultures originating from India, the Middle East, and Orthodox Muslim regions (coincidentally, where the consumption of alcoholic beverages is prohibited). More recently, this cultural practice has become a noncultural social activity among young adults in the United States and Europe in the form of hookah lounges. In municipalities with tobacco bans, establishments have permits for tobacco consumption as hookah lounges or cigar bars. In both cases, other products including alcoholic beverages are also sold to generate additional revenue.

Some mainstream religions currently use small quantities of alcoholic beverages or alcohol vessels as symbolic gestures from biblical or Talmudic stories. They do not support consumption to the point of intoxication. Many ancient societies, however, use plant-derived substances at doses that purposely put the participant into an altered state. The scientific word for such substances is *entheogen* and was coined as a replacement word for *hallucinogen* or *psychedelic*, but only when used as part of a religious or spiritual practice.

Cultural Differences in the Use of Alcohol

Misinformation and exaggerations about cultural differences in the use of alcohol abound in society. Here are a few dubious beliefs:

- Irish have the highest incidence of alcoholism in the world.
- Native Americans and First Nations tribes have a uniformly high rate of alcoholism.
- There are relationships between the early use of alcohol in families and the rate of alcoholism. For example, Italians have a low rate of alcoholism because of the family use of wine with meals, whereas cultures without a history of family alcohol use have high rates of alcoholism.
- Heavy drinking in a society means there will be a higher incidence of alcoholism.
- Rates of alcoholism are low in Saudi Arabia, due to a low genetic vulnerability to alcoholism.

Generally, none of the above has been proved by scientific studies, and a few have been disproved. Much of the confusion comes from the broad, general use of the word *alcoholism* in cases that actually involve only "heavy drinking." Recall the discussion in Chapter 1 pointing out the difference between alcohol (drug) "abuse" and alcohol (chemical) "dependence." Scientifically, "alcoholism" is actually "alcohol dependence," and it involves only a relatively small percentage (15%) of drinkers, and not all heavy drinkers are alcohol dependent.

Thus, when someone mentions "Irish drinking," this is thought to be a joke and people begin to laugh. In actuality, one study has indicated that the English have a higher rate of alcohol dependence than the Irish. Also, studies of alcohol dependence in different Native American tribes have clearly shown that although the rate of drinking is high, the rates of alcohol dependence vary among the tribes. Finally, we now know that with Saudis who travel to and live in the United States and adapt to the American culture, if they begin drinking, the rate of alcohol dependence can be as high as that of Americans'. Thus, new studies of "alcoholism" are showing that what was thought to be alcoholism is really only heavy drinking, and the actual rate of the disease of alcohol dependence can be much different. This conclusion is now possible with the emerging diagnostic principles described in Chapter 1 relating to *DSM-IV-TR* (2000) differences between alcohol abuse and alcohol dependence.

While studies on gender and cultural differences regarding alcohol and other drugs are fairly abundant, there is still a lack of total understanding about how gender and culture affect drug use and its outcomes. This is an area where new research is badly needed.

CHAPTER 10

Major Mental Illnesses Accompanying Drug Use Disorders

with Peter J. Pociluyko, MA, CASAC, CCS

PATIENTS' OVERVIEW

Axis I (major) mental disorders are damaging to patients when they occur alone. When occurring with drug use, an important question is, Did the mental disorder cause the drug use? If this is the case, removing the symptoms of the mental disorder might cause drug problems to diminish or go away. On the other hand, what if excessive drug use led to symptoms of mental disorder such as depression or anxiety? This chapter focuses on the more important issues of making a proper diagnosis, formulating a clear treatment plan, and then making sure that the treatment plan is followed. What we find in many cases is that upon removal of the drug, co-occurring disorders get better.

A few common factors affect Axis I disorder comorbidity with drugs

- They are chronic diseases affecting the brain and neurobiology.
- They are disorders that affect judgment, cognition, emotions, and behavior.
- The development of each disorder is influenced by genetic, psychological, behavioral, and social factors.

- They involve common chemical pathways, for example, dopamine, serotonin, glutamate, GABA.
- They usually require periods of intensive multifaceted treatment.
- As with any chronic disease, relapse is common.
- They require lifelong management to keep the disease under control.
- They are disorders that require reliance on medicines, sometimes for long periods.
- They involve use of the same psychological defenses to avoid problem recognition and change.
- They are adversely impacted by Axis II disorders (personality disorders).

Major Depression Compared to Dysthymic Disorder

Major depression and dysthymic disorder must be differentiated from normal periods of sadness, sadness due to change or loss, grief reactions, and periods of low mood and agitation—symptoms that are experienced during early recovery, as well. Short bouts of mild to moderate depressed mood and sadness are normal in recovery, along with insomnia, irritability, and minor aches and pains. Major depression involves a cluster of five or more core symptoms that have been present for at least 2 or more weeks or for months or years. These include loss of pleasure, feelings of sadness, sleep disturbances (insomnia, too little sleep, or constant sleep), weight gain or loss, increase or decrease in appetite, fatigue, lack of concentration, feeling that one's actions and thoughts are slowed down, chronic irritability, feelings of hopelessness, and thoughts of suicide.

Dysthymic disorder contains a similar spectrum of symptoms as listed above, but these symptoms are of a low grade and present for a long period of time (over 6 months and not uncommon to be present for years before diagnosis, if a diagnosis is ever made). Such symptoms (hopelessness, hypersomnia, lack of concentration, low energy, irritability, changes in appetite) are dismissed by family, colleagues, and friends as symptoms of a person being "moody" or "stressed."

The difference between periodic bouts of sadness and major depression versus dysthymic disorder requires knowing the frequency, severity, intensity, duration, and number of symptoms as described in *DSM-IV-TR* (2000). Many patients with major depression or dysthymic disorder may not appear overtly depressed but are identified by other symptoms such as chronic negative mood, irritability, inability to focus on or recall details, chronic feelings of anxiety, and chronic pain, especially in the back, neck, or legs, headaches, or gastrointestinal difficulties. About half of people with a diagnosis of major depression also have an anxiety disorder. In fact, co-occurring anxiety disorders and depressive disorders are so common that it has led to theories that these conditions have similar causes.

Alcohol, cannabis, and stimulants are commonly used to relieve depression symptoms. As with most co-occurring disorders, a large percentage of depressed people smoke tobacco because both nicotine and the social activity of smoking are perceived to lift mood, reduce anxiety, and reduce feelings of stress. However, depressants can produce a dose- and duration-related rebound effect of agitation, and stimulants can produce dose- and duration-related rebound depression. Tobacco is a stimulant and while it may temporarily provide a mood lift and relieve anxiety related to nicotine withdrawal, tobacco smoke aggravates and directly causes depression and anxiety. Use of these drugs makes symptoms of depression worse. For women, smoking tobacco increases the risk of major depression by 93% and tobacco use has been implicated as a contributing factor to depression and anxiety.

Symptoms of depression in drug users are often dismissed and believed to be recovery-related or drug-induced; however, with any drug use disorder or co-occurring disorder, this is not accurate. Postrecovery symptoms of depression that do not subside after modest exercise, or after attending counseling sessions or fellowship meetings, should be evaluated. Practitioners need not wait several months after recovery begins before attempting to diagnose depression. Whenever a patient's symptoms are severe, prolonged (more than 2 weeks), or have frequent recurrence, it should be assumed that the condition is more than drug use or recovery-related. Antidepressant drugs are necessary and do not compromise recovery; in fact, unresolved depression raises the risk of relapse. The treatment of depression results in significant relief from anxiety (another symptom of depression) and chronic pain, especially musculoskeletal pain. Because unmanaged anxiety and pain are significant stress factors, failure to treat either symptom significantly increases the risk of relapse. Pain, anxiety, and depression compound the risk of suicide.

Bipolar and Cyclothymic Disorder

Drug abuse patients with concurrent bipolar or cyclothymic disorder are one of the most commonly misdiagnosed and untreated subgroups of dual diagnosis patients. Patients may have bipolar type 1 disorder or bipolar type 2 disorder, or a milder form called cyclothymic disorder.

Cyclothymic disorder is similar to bipolar disorder but the periods of mania are not as severe or as common.

One estimate is that people with bipolar illness have a 60%–75% risk of developing a drug abuse disorder over their lifetimes. Among people with psychiatric illness, bipolar patients have the second highest rate of drug use disorders at 61%, compared with 47% for those with schizophrenia, 27% for those with major depressive disorder, and 84% for those with antisocial personality disorder (APD). In some cases, a prolonged use of stimulants, psychedelics, or even steroids may promote the onset of bipolar illness in susceptible individuals (National Alliance on Mental Illness, 2010). This risk is especially related to the use of MDMA (ecstasy), amphetamine, or cocaine. Many people like to use stimulants, even though this makes their mania worse because they strongly desire the energy, the feeling of power and invincibility, and the euphoria. People with bipolar illness also use alcohol (or may use antianxiety drugs such as benzodiazepines) to lift their mood during depressive periods, to reduce their feelings of anxiety, and to curb excess manic behavior. Stimulants may also be abused during the depressive phase of bipolar illness.

During manic phases, bipolar patients tend to have a euphoric, grandiose sense of importance, with grossly exaggerated self-regard and extreme narcissism. They become easily agitated, angry, and even violent if prevented from doing what they want to do. Mania and lack of sleep may lead to paranoid thinking and fears of being harmed by others. These symptoms are made worse if the person uses stimulant or psychedelic drugs, which can cause paranoid ideation and drug-induced psychosis. The risk of suicide is very high during periods of mixed symptoms of depression and mania, or during depression. However, during periods of mania, behavior is self-destructive in the form of gambling or compulsive spending. Such individuals develop excess elation, grandiosity, and delusional thinking that lead to errors in judgment, resulting in serious injury or death (e.g., the person thinking it possible to jump or fly from a great height and land safely).

Bipolar disorder and cyclothymic disorder can be misdiagnosed as major depression because prior symptoms of mania may have not been recognized, or there is no reported history suggesting mania or hypomania. All drug use disorder patients, especially those with a history of depression, should be carefully screened for a history of mania or hypomania symptoms. In general, bipolar symptoms are present by the age of 30, but there are cases in which the onset of the illness does not occur until the person is much older. As with alcohol dependence, there is a genetic risk for developing bipolar disorder. Most individuals with bipolar illness will show a positive family history of depression, manic behavior, or psychiatric hospitalization. Patients with repeated episodes of depression are not fully evaluated for an undiagnosed bipolar disorder, and it is especially important to ask about any recent or past family history of the illness. A positive family history is more useful to identifying bipolar disorder than an assessment of patient symptoms alone.

Drug Use Disorder, Mental Disorder, and Suicide Risk

A suicide attempt is a deliberate effort to kill oneself. Patients who are more serious about suicide will have a detailed plan with a lethal method and a time, date, and place in mind. The more detailed and specific the plan, the greater the risk. Depression, anxiety, and hopelessness are key factors behind suicide and the risk is elevated by episodes of mania and psychosis.

Suicidal ideation and suicide attempts are a significant concern for people with drug use and mental disorders. A meta-analysis of many studies for U.S. and international populations showed that people with alcohol, opioid, mixed drug use, and use of drugs by injection had a risk for suicide that was 9 times higher than the norm. It also showed that people being treated for drug use disorders are at increased risk for suicide.

It is important that treatment professionals regularly assess patients for suicide risk, especially those with anxiety, chronic pain, history of bipolar disorders, and depression. The rate of suicide attempts across personality disorders is similar to the rate of those with mood disorders.

Suicide risk does not automatically disappear with abstinence from drugs or a remission of the most severe mental symptoms. During recovery from a drug use disorder, the risk of suicide is generally high in the first 2 years of recovery. Patients with co-occurring disorders in general have very elevated risks of suicide due to frequent histories of instability with managing their symptoms, jobs, and relationships, feeling isolated, experiencing severe and prolonged depression, and struggling with unmanaged anxiety.

Acute attempts to commit suicide are precipitated by an overwhelming single crisis, such as the loss of a spouse. A chronic pattern of attempting suicide or suicide gestures suggests long-standing and untreated symptoms of depression, anxiety, or pain. These feelings can also be amplified when a relapse occurs. It is common for patients to attempt suicide during or after a relapse, because they may believe they have failed one more time. Suicide is also a way to avoid feeling like a failure, or to stop feeling depression, anxiety, and pain.

Alcohol and drug abuse are second only to major depression and major mood disorders as high risk factors for suicide. Compared to the general population, the suicide risk is 6 times higher for alcohol and drug abusers. However, suicide is also a great risk during the first and second years of recovery. For people who have a co-occurring mood disorder, such as major depression, the risk is further increased.

Alcoholics and opioid-dependent patients are prone to depression and have an equally high degree of suicide risk both during active use and in the first year of recovery. Stimulant users are most prone to suicide right after a period of prolonged stimulant use because of abstinence-related depression. Patients with co-occurring mental disorders such as schizophrenia and bipolar illness have a higher-than-normal risk for suicide.

Some very depressed patients feel such low psychological and physical energy that they won't attempt suicide during this phase. Some say they are feeling "dead, empty, tired of living, or lost." This group is at major suicide risk when their depression begins to lift, such as when treated with an antidepressant. A patient's rapid or sudden change from severe depression to a calm, positive, or mildly elated mood should be a concern for family and medical practitioners. This mood lift may indicate that the person has reconciled his or her ambivalence about dying, plans for life to end, and feels that relief is near.

Anxiety Disorders

Many co-occurring disorder patients will report symptoms of anxiety related to recovery. Reports of anxiety, restlessness, and general fears (along with depression) are so common among addiction patients that many addiction professionals assume it is normal or it is a patient's defensive response about change. Other mental health practitioners tend to consider anxiety a primary concern, and will suspect that symptoms of a mental disorder are reemerging or are part of an anxiety disorder. When anxiety symptoms are significant, frequent, and prolonged, it may suggest an anxiety disorder, posttraumatic stress disorder (PTSD), major depression, dysthymic disorder, or some combination thereof. In fact, chronic episodes of anxiety are a sign of chronic pain, depression, or an untreated medical condition. Unrelenting anxiety is a major factor that prompts people to attempt and commit suicide.

Anxiety from drug withdrawal is common in patients who abruptly stop using alcohol, drugs, and tobacco. Anxiety can also be related to self-recognition of limitations, personal deficits, and recognition of past behavior that harmed or disappointed others. Anxiety that is primarily related to change and loss (grief of having to give up the drug) will usually diminish once a patient talks about these fears during counseling or in a fellowship meeting. Acute anxiety, panic attacks, and unremitting episodes of anxiety typically have other causes besides drug withdrawal and should not be dismissed. Hypoglycemia, thyroid disorders, cardiac arrhythmias, and early symptoms of a heart attack are examples of many medical conditions that are known to have psychological symptoms of dread and acute anxiety, and they need to be ruled out.

Panic disorders have a strong biological basis and result in overwhelming fear and dread, along with physical symptoms of sweating, weakness, faintness, rapid heart rate, and hyperventilation. Symptoms that increase in intensity and become more frequent, chronic pain, depression, and any history of violence, combat, sexual abuse, or witnessing of trauma can also produce anxiety. Chronic anxiety and panic disorders raise glucocorticoid levels (stress hormones), putting the body in a state of hyperalertness as if about to fight, flee, or freeze. This condition puts patients at greater risk for other illnesses, especially if their symptoms are not managed. Patients with chronic anxiety tend to develop stress-related physiological disorders and are at greater risk for depression and suicide.

The use of caffeine, found in many over-the-counter medications, coffee, tea, energy drinks, and carbonated sodas, is a common cause of inability to sleep, agitation, unknown restlessness, and mild anxiety. In susceptible people, even small doses of 75–100 mg of caffeine (equal to a cup of coffee or a bottle of soda) can precipitate anxiety or panic attacks. Tobacco use, especially in the form of heavy smoking (20 or more cigarettes per day), increases general anxiety and increases the risk for panic attacks and agoraphobia (fear of being in confined spaces; feeling of being trapped; fear of panicking).

Tobacco-induced anxiety should not be confused with anxiety caused by nicotine withdrawal. When people with a drug use disorder or mental disorder try to stop smoking tobacco, they confuse the symptoms of tobacco withdrawal with general anxiety, panic attacks, or symptoms of an existing mental disorder. Chronic use of tobacco actually increases feelings of anxiety. Many users feel anxiety, restlessness, and tension from nicotine withdrawal, and incorrectly think that because these symptoms are relieved when they smoke, tobacco is providing anxiety relief and helping them control their symptoms. Smoking tobacco only stops anxiety related to nicotine withdrawal; chronic tobacco use, however, increases feelings of anxiety. Tobacco use, especially in the form of daily tobacco smoking, is also a risk factor for panic disorder, agoraphobia, and generalized anxiety disorder.

Schizophrenia and Drug Use Disorder

Schizophrenia and the related disorders of schizophreniform and schizo-affective disorders are psychotic disorders characterized by "positive" symptoms that reflect an excess or distortion of normal functions and "negative" symptoms that reflect a reduction or loss of normal functions. Positive symptoms include disturbed thinking, loosely connected ideas or thoughts, disorganized behavior, delusions, and hallucinations, usually of an auditory nature (hearing voices). Negative symptoms include flat affect, depression, lack of motivation, lack of feeling pleasure, inability to speak or communicate clearly, and social withdrawal. Symptoms will typically appear in adolescence or early adulthood; however, it is possible for some people to have a very late onset of the disorder and not show symptoms until they are well into their 30s or 40s. In general, patients with these illnesses are among the most difficult to engage and retain in treatment for their drug use problems.

A useful way for addiction professionals to identify key *negative* symptoms of schizophrenia is using the "Five As." These patients generally show negative symptoms in most of these areas:

- Avolition—pervasive lack of initiative or motivation, including taking care of activities or daily living and basic needs
- Autistic behavior—withdrawal into their own world and showing limited response to stimuli or other people
- Affect—flat facial affect (emotional expression) or extreme opposite emotions such as feeling happy and sad at the same time
- Alogia—difficulty with speech or inability to speak
- Anhedonia—a loss of interest or pleasure

The diagnosis of schizophrenia, according to *DSM-IV-TR (2000)*, requires at least a 1-month duration of two or more *positive* symptoms, unless hallucinations or delusions are especially bizarre, in which case one positive symptom alone will support a diagnosis. Negative symptoms are difficult to evaluate because they are not as grossly abnormal as positive symptoms and may be caused by a variety of other factors (e.g., social withdrawal may be an adaptation to a persecutory delusion). Older antipsychotic medications tend to produce side effects that can resemble the negative symptoms of flat affect and avolition, which is why some patients discontinue these medications. Some of the new-generation medications are better at reducing these negative symptoms.

Diagnoses of schizophrenia and limited symptoms of schizophrenia have occurred among a number of teenagers and young adults with histories of using so-called designer drugs, stimulants, and marijuana, but also with less commonly used psychedelics such as LSD and dissociative anesthetics such as phencyclidine (PCP) and ketamine. For susceptible individuals, use of these drugs can precipitate the earlier onset of schizophrenic symptoms and will make an existing disorder worse.

People with schizophrenia may use alcohol, nicotine, or other psychoactive drugs to reduce unpleasant auditory hallucinations (e.g., hearing voices that say, "You are a terrible person") and to control acute or prolonged anxiety—what many describe as "psychic pain." Schizophrenics also use illicit and prescription drugs to reduce anxiety and stress, and commonly will become daily and heavy tobacco users. Alcohol and sedatives such as diazepam (Valium) are their common drugs. Opioids temporarily reduce some symptoms of schizophrenia, and many people with this disorder will by accident recognize they can keep some symptoms under control by using opioids. Patients with opioid dependence may have unrecognized schizophrenia until they are detoxed, or after gradually reducing their methadone dose. Nicotine and possibly other chemicals in tobacco smoke provide mild improvements in focus and cognition, and help overcome some of the negative symptoms such as depressed mood and anhedonia. After using nicotine for a while, these individuals may also need to use tobacco to ward off nicotine withdrawal symptoms, which include anxiety, agitation, and unease. Less commonly understood is that tobacco use directly increases anxiety, increases the risk of depression and social phobias, and actually can make psychiatric symptoms worse.

PTSD and Drug Abuse

PTSD is an anxiety disorder characterized by a variety of symptoms occurring after at least one severe traumatic event. The patient may have been the victim of a physical attack, sexual assault, or robbery, may have engaged in or witnessed combat, may have been involved in a shoot-out, or may have been a victim of a serious accident. People can develop symptoms after witnessing a traumatic event (e.g., children who observe murders or domestic violence) and may develop symptoms due to psychological rehearsal of the event. Many co-occurring disorder patients have also experienced traumatic events prior to or after the onset of a drug use disorder or another mental disorder.

An individual who has experienced a recent traumatic event may not initially show symptoms or may only present minimal symptoms, sometimes for weeks or months after the event. Many people who have PTSD report that their symptoms began and then increased in intensity and frequency, shortly after a traumatic event(s). Initial symptoms include acute feelings of helplessness, fear, and self-doubt that are accompanied by nightmares. Others report the "reliving" of the event, over and over, and seek escape from these intrusive recollections. Many people with PTSD will try to consciously suppress intrusive thoughts, images, or remembrances and try to distract themselves from unpleasant emotions and memories. As symptoms progress, this usually leads to increased levels of anxiety, a state of hypervigilance (increased awareness, expressed as easily provoked anger or aggression), an inability to concentrate, depression, and sleeplessness. This is followed by the development of feelings of depersonalization (numbness), floating or out-of-body sensations, social phobias—and may include paranoia and panic attacks. These symptoms can easily mimic other mental disorders, drug use disorders, drug relapse, or symptoms of early recovery. PTSD and borderline personality disorder (BPD) can look very similar and be confused with each other. The symptoms are so alike that PTSD is sometimes referred to as a close cousin of BPD.

After a trauma people first try to use the normal defense mechanisms of denial and suppression to manage unpleasant thoughts and feelings. When simple defenses do not work, patients switch to dissociation. This can be an effective temporary coping tool and is a normal response to an abnormal event. The problem occurs when this method is generalized into a primary response to any situation involving perceived stress. People who begin to have symptoms related to trauma start to say things to themselves, such as *This isn't really happening to me* and they try to divorce or "split off" their feelings from their memories. Once people try to split off feelings, sensations, or memories, the result is that they end up disowning some aspect of the experience. This leads to internal dialogue, such as *This is not really happening to me,* and they may begin saying to themselves things such as *I do not feel anger. I do not feel attractive, I do not feel sexual desire*. In response to the dissociation and disownment, people may begin to devalue themselves or their own feelings: *"Anger is bad," "Sexual feelings are bad," "Attraction to others is bad."*

Individuals with traumatic experiences and the resulting painful feelings and intrusive thoughts from the trauma commonly use alcohol, sedative drugs, opioids, or cannabis to counter any intrusive visual or auditory memories of the event, as well as to curb their bouts of panic, general anxiety, and sleeplessness. However, drug use can result in unintended effects that complicate the original symptoms of PTSD. For example, alcohol can relieve anxiety and help a person sleep, yet it produces a "physiological rebound effect" after the drug has worn off. The depressant effects of other depressants are also followed by rebound agitation, irritability, and anxiety, and the use of stimulants is followed by rebound depression. As with any mental disorder, a rebound effect is generally duration- and dose-dependent, meaning that the more the person uses at one time, and the longer this period of use continues, the greater the drug effect and the greater the drug rebound effect. A rebound effect may exaggerate PTSD symptoms, aggravate any other mental disorder, and tend to lead to more drug use or result in a drug use disorder. Cannabis can produce temporary sedation but also can cause ego-fragmentation, leading to feelings of depersonalization, anxiety, and—in especially susceptible individuals—paranoia.

Many people who suffer from PTSD begin to use or increase their tobacco use, believing that tobacco "calms their nerves." Heavy tobacco use has long been observed as associated with PTSD, and nicotine is used to decrease physiological arousal and to overcome feelings of numbness, detachment, and depression. Specifically with combat veterans diagnosed with PTSD, heavy smoking positively correlates with increased PTSD symptoms. Recent observations with combat veterans suggest that tobacco use can aggravate PTSD symptoms. This is because nicotine appears to increase the vividness of memories, resulting in a reexperiencing of the trauma.

Adolescents With Co-occurring Disorders

Drug use and mental disorders frequently have an early age of onset, beginning during adolescence. The median age for onset of a childhood anxiety disorder is about 11 years, whereas the median age for the onset of a drug use disorder is usually 20 years. Either disorder can become persistent or disabling when not treated early. While alcohol and marijuana are seen as the main drugs leading to drug use disorder, these can also support and complicate the symptoms of a mental disorder. Furthermore, tobacco and alcohol use during adolescence appears to be a key factor in the adult development of drug use disorder and mental disorder.

Some research indicates that as many as 80% of adolescents diagnosed with alcohol abuse or alcohol dependence are suffering from a mood disorder (dysthymic disorder, bipolar disorder, or major depression), ADHD, anxiety disorder, or conduct disorder (CD). Drug abuse disorders may develop in concert with a mental disorder, after a mental disorder, or prior to a mental disorder. Too often the focus is upon which came first, is cloaked as a diagnostic issue, and in state-operated programs can be a funding question to determine which public agency should treat the child. Knowing which disorder occurred first is generally not important in the treatment of these conditions, although some experts believe that the disorder that occurred first is more likely to be the probable cause of the second disorder.

Many risk factors influence the development of mental disorders and drug abuse among young people. Adolescents must manage a number of developmental issues and pressures that increases their risk to use drugs, and early drug use increases the risk of developing a mental disorder. At the same time, an emerging mental disorder can precede and substantially increase the risk of developing a drug use disorder. Youth from socially and economically disadvantaged backgrounds have an elevated risk of mental health disorders and drug use disorders. Adolescence is also a key period of brain development, which generally continues until about age 21–24. During this period, important neural connections are occurring between the primitive brain structures (brain stem, cerebellum, and mesocortex) that control basic emotions and cravings, and the neocortex (cerebrum and cerebral cortex), which controls inhibitions, thinking, judgment, and rationality. The use of drugs during this period can lead to undeveloped neural connections. A failure to develop a strong inhibitory control over cravings and emotions during this period is a factor in the development of mental disorder and drug use disorder during adolescence or young adulthood.

Tobacco Dependence and Co-occurring Disorders

The issue of tobacco dependence is highlighted in this chapter for many important reasons. Among people with depression and anxiety disorders, between 40% and 50% smoke, about double the rate of the general population. Smoking and especially heavy smoking is increasingly seen in people with PTSD, especially among veterans of combat.

Within addiction and mental health treatment settings, tobacco use has too often been viewed as a minor concern when compared to disorders involving alcohol; stimulant, cannabis, or opioid use; or a mental disorder. Frequently, tobacco use is seen as a "latter concern" that should only be addressed if the patient has serious life-threatening illness requiring immediate abstinence, such as recent myocardial infarction, stroke, severe hypertension, or chronic obstructive pulmonary disease (COPD).

Tobacco use has significant emotional, psychological, and behavioral cues for prompting the use of other drugs. The recognition that tobacco use increased the desire to use alcohol was noted in 1798 by physician and signer of the Declaration of Independence, Benjamin Rush. Tobacco

Addiction Essentials

users, especially people who smoke tobacco, are overrepresented among people who have drug use disorders and mental disorders. People with dependence or a mental disorder are 2–3 times more likely to smoke tobacco than the general population. In fact, those with a mental health or drug use disorder consume 44% of all cigarettes sold in the United States (Nicotine Quick Facts, 2010). Between 75% and 95% of people with schizophrenia smoke. In people with drug or alcohol use problems, the rate of tobacco use ranges from 75% to 100%. Of the 435,000 annual smoking-related deaths in the United States, at least 200,000 are people with mental health or drug use disorders. Thus, approximately 200,000 people with mental illness or dependence die each year from tobacco-related illnesses. Some studies have shown that people with serious mental illness die on average 25 years earlier than the general population, primarily due to smoking-related illness. People with drug use disorders who smoke are much more likely to die from tobacco use than from associated drug or alcohol dependence, even when the drug or alcohol problem was resolved (Nicotine Quick Facts, 2010).

Tobacco can be thought of as the "drug of choice" for most patients, because it is the drug usually used first. It is the drug most are unwilling to stop, and it is the drug they always return to using. Hence, when patients stop alcohol, stimulants, or opioids, but continue to smoke tobacco, research has shown the risk of relapse is greater; the risk of relapse decreases when people stop using tobacco. Ironically, many early addiction treatment pioneers of the late 1800s to 1920s noted that tobacco use was a major "addiction," and it was addressed along with all other drug use because continued tobacco use increased the relapse back to alcohol and opioids. However, the recognition of this relationship was lost for many decades.

CHAPTER 11

Personality Disorders and Drug Use

with Peter J. Pociluyko, MA, CASAC, CCS

PATIENTS' OVERVIEW

Among individuals with severe psychological traits and personality disorders, drug use is associated with exaggerated behavior, such as anger, impulsivity, aggression, or paranoia. Those with personality disorders, in fact, seek drugs to medicate their symptoms. The obvious solution for such individuals involves treatment for drug use disorders, along with counseling to get at the heart of the personality disorder and those who have rigid traits and defenses.

Personality provides a sense of stability and predictability about a person, and this stability is related to embedded traits or psychological qualities. A personality trait is an innate, predictable, psychological quality or characteristic (thinking processes, perceptual ability, emotional reactions) that is stable and does not easily change. Normally personality traits are functional, many traits are common across people, and they will vary in strength from person to person.

While co-occurring Axis I mental disorders and drug use disorders are viewed as the more serious conditions for treatment, the concurrent presence of an Axis II disorder (such as personality disorders) can be equally severe and present challenging, time- and effort-intensive situations with patients. Many people with personality disorders will have one or more Axis I mental disorder and drug use disorder diagnoses, and it is fairly common for patients with Axis I disorders to also have a personality disorder (formerly known as "character disorder").

A personality disorder is diagnosed when a person has ingrained, rigid personality traits that repeatedly result in dysfunctional cognitive, behavioral, and emotional functioning plus maladaptive behaviors. These patients are not psychotic (though they may deteriorate under severe stress or in confinement). Instead they have erratic and odd psychological qualities and troublesome interpersonal patterns. Their personality traits include impulsivity, being unable to tolerate and contain anxiety, and a lack of insight and self-awareness about the impact of their behavior. They are usually narcissistic, and may have significant confusion of identity or an overly rigid sense of identity. Their ego-defenses are also more rigid than those of other patients.

It is important to understand that people with personality disorders have primary maladaptive psychological traits that are independent of their drug use or mental health disorder symptoms. Drug overuse readily magnifies psychiatric symptoms and innate personality qualities, but also reduces certain symptoms. At the same time, abstinence will not automatically cause maladaptive personality traits to subside or disappear. In fact, abstinence will usually appear to intensify their maladaptive personality traits. These maladaptive psychological qualities and behaviors can look like active drug use, and make it difficult to focus on treating the patient's drug use disorder.

Types of Personality Disorder
Personality disorders are grouped into three clusters:

- Those with Cluster A personality disorders tend to withdraw from others and are the least likely to overuse chemicals, although alcohol overuse is not unusual and tobacco dependence is very common. These categories include schizotypal (signs of schizophrenia), paranoid, and schizoid personality disorders.
- Those with Cluster B disorders are emotionally erratic, are impulsive, can appear irrational, have frequent irresponsibility for their own behavior, and have a common pattern of exploiting others. This group is most likely to develop a co-occurring drug use disorder; will present significant interpersonal conflict with family, social services, and the legal system; and are usually man-

dated into treatment. This group includes antisocial personality disorder (APD), borderline personality disorder (BPD), narcissistic personality disorder (NPD), histrionic (attention-seeking) personality disorder (HPD), and the unclassified passive-aggressive personality disorder. People with Cluster B personality disorders are most likely to willfully use to excess or become dependent on alcohol and other psychoactive drugs. They actively seek and use pleasure-producing drugs to gain relief from anxiety, depression, and boredom and to manage and expel their feelings of psychological chaos.

• Those with Cluster C disorders tend to accommodate to the wants of others and try to avoid conflict. While they have a risk for using sedatives, alcohol, and antianxiety drugs to manage their internal anxiety, they are not common in addiction treatment, but may present in a mental health center. Cluster C includes people with avoidant disorder, dependent disorder, and obsessive-compulsive personality disorder (OCD).

Challenges of Diagnosis and Treatment

One of the challenges of using *DSM-IV-TR* (2000) criteria is that all disorders are classified by a cluster of behavioral signs and patient symptoms (complaints of distress). Some experts argue that the diagnosis of a personality disorder requires behavioral signs and symptoms, plus evidence of specific maladaptive personality (psychological) traits. In practice, one should see both maladaptive traits and corresponding maladaptive behaviors. Their psychological traits (such as ways of perceiving, interpretations of others' behavior, reactions, and beliefs) will feel normal (ego-syntonic) to the patient. They view external events or other people as the cause of all their problems. It is only when their psychological traits and behaviors cause distress or feel alien (ego-dystonic or out of character) that they seek treatment. However, once their feelings of anxiety, boredom, or depression lift, and the state of distress ceases, these patients will tend to abandon treatment or become disruptive until discharged from a program.

Many people with personality disorders can function well given reasonable structure, such as a routine work schedule or an organized work setting, or when allowed to apply their maladaptive traits to work settings. Problems emerge when they must regularly relate to other people or deal with major changes in work or family life, and when they rely on psychoactive drugs to manage feelings of chaos, anxiety, boredom, or hostility.

Borderline Personality Disorder (BPD)

BPD is characterized by instability of mood, behavior, relationships, and self-image. Some refer to this condition as unstable or cycloid, believing that the term *BPD* is not descriptive and implies a pejorative connotation.

BPD is common among drug use disorder and mental disorder patients, but must be distinguished from recovery-related symptoms, medical conditions, and Axis I disorders such as posttraumatic stress disorder (PTSD) or bipolar disorder. There is increasing speculation that BPD may actually be an Axis I mood disorder, similar to bipolar disorder. BPD readily mimics and is often confused with PTSD, bipolar disorder, cyclothymic disorder, and the rare dissociative identity disorder. It is not uncommon for a person with BPD to also have PTSD or bipolar disorder or both.

Symptoms of BPD include emotional instability with significant shifts in mood; inappropriate or uncontrollable anger; self-harming behavior, such as drug overdose, compulsive spending, or sexual promiscuity; and chaotic, intense relationships characterized by "splitting." The term *splitting* does not mean "dividing or splitting staff against each other"; rather, it is a defense to rigidly separate positive and negative thoughts, feelings, and ideas about any person—for example, viewing a counselor as completely negative and untrustworthy, then a day later as completely positive and trustworthy. Splitting occurs because people with BPD have trouble tolerating opposing emotional states. Patients often make recurrent suicidal threats, gestures, and attempts. These people will demonstrate frantic responses to actual or perceived abandonment or even innocuous behavior that they perceive as abandonment. They have remarkable identity confusion, illustrated by a persistent uncertainty about their own self-image, sexuality, and personal values. Because they lack a clear sense of identity, they readily assume "new identities" and become "identity chameleons," taking on new roles as if on a theater stage. Assuming new identities is an effort to appear and feel psychologically stable and to overcome their negative self-images and chronic feelings of emptiness and anxiety. Patients with BPD have been known to quickly assume symptoms of someone else's condition or to provide symptom histories of other patients.

The overuse of chemicals, taking other people's medications, suicidal gestures, abstinence followed by many relapses, transient psychotic states, and paranoia are common in these patients, especially when they are under stress.

Antisocial Personality Disorder (APD)

Drug use disorder is very common among people with APD. Those with

APD have a history of pervasive lying (often for no reason), theft, assaults, legal violations, broken promises, serial relationships, and sexual promiscuity. They seek power over others, are impulsive, have little empathy, and are exploitive. They readily project (attribute) their own hostile feelings and motives onto others, and then provoke a fight or argument with them. Their antisocial thinking and behavior generally become less controlled as drug use problems progress. They view the main cause of their difficulties as others getting in the way of their desires. Chemical dependency professionals frequently confuse patients with this disorder with patients who merely display frequent antisocial behavior when under the influence. There is a difference between patients who have primary antisocial personality traits and behavior (with biopsychogenic origins) and people who display secondary antisocial behavior and traits induced by drug use disorder. Many people with APD are not involved in the criminal justice system and only an estimated 30%–40% (those who are not socially successful) come into conflict with the law. People with mild forms of APD can be highly functional, seeking jobs in the military, security, police, and business, and may have no history of problems with the authorities unless they develop drug or alcohol problems. People with APD have been identified as having low cortical arousal, and as a result they seek intense stimulation by performing daring and thrill-seeking behaviors. Alcohol, sedative, opioid, and stimulant drug use amplifies their underlying impulsivity, hostility, and egotistical thinking and increases their aggressive behavior. For example, bar room brawls are more common after alcohol has been consumed in these individuals. They are prone to violating program rules, missing sessions, or abandoning treatment, even if mandated.

Histrionic Personality Disorder (HPD)
Individuals with HPD demonstrate lots of flirtatiousness, dramatic behavior, and vanity while being demanding and manipulative. They constantly seek approval and attention and hate being alone. They often appear like "model patients," as if fully compliant with treatment and recovery, yet they are not. They are usually extroverted, socially skilled, and well liked. Notably they do not pay attention to important details, they dislike routine, or when demands are placed upon them, they are quick to change their minds. They also actively avoid any discussion or recollection that is unpleasant. During treatment they are prone to give vague details, change the subject if it is unpleasant or painful, and give excessive compliments to the practitioner or fellow patients. They are highly conscious of their dress and appearance, and use seductive be-

havior. Some will focus on physical ailments and somatic complaints to get attention.

People with HPD are usually interested in novelty and easily become bored, and then move on to a new interest, often a new person of interest. They actively seek out new personal relationships through fellowship groups or treatment groups; they are prone to compulsive sexual behavior and to having serial partners. During educational, group, or family treatment sessions they will often insist on being the center of attention and may become agitated or depressed if not given sufficient attention. They usually enter treatment under some mandate in order to avoid confinement, job loss, or sanctions. However, if they are voluntary patients, they usually have depression, anxiety, and impaired control over drug use. Once their symptoms have subsided, they are quick to abandon treatment.

Narcissistic Personality Disorder (NPD)

NPD individuals have high ambition, entertain grandiose fantasy, and depend on admiration and acclaim from others. They share many personality traits with APD individuals. They view themselves as special and expect others to publicly express admiration for their alleged "special qualities." They believe the rules of civility, treatment programs, or the courts do not apply to them. Typically they have a pattern of exploitation and ruthlessness, and have little empathy for others. If others express pain, sadness, and feeling hurt or disappointment, this is viewed by these individuals as a weakness. They are motivated by having "special status," receiving admiration, and gaining power over others. One of their patterns is to find fault with others, while calling attention to their own "virtues" and abilities. A second pattern is to provoke conflict among others because they enjoy watching others in conflict (a vicarious way to expel their internal feelings of conflict and chaos). They are also prone to having depression, anxiety disorders, and stress–induced disorders.

When they become abstinent, they tend to complain more often than other patients, routinely insist on exceptions to the rules, and find fault with others (staff, family members, and patients). As with APD, they will repeatedly fail to recognize their complicity in their own failure and interpersonal conflict. It often takes longer than usual to help them gain insight and learn from their mistakes. Their efforts to be viewed as special, admired, and holding power over others will be as pronounced or even stronger when they are abstinent than when they were using. They can be very intelligent and hard working, and present an image of being self-assured, competent, and successful. However, these personality traits and their self-assured behavior cloak intense fears of uncertainty, feelings of personal dissatisfaction, and feelings of inferiority. They accept their idealized qualities and reject all the qualities they dislike, which they project (attribute) to others, and then criticize others for those undesirable qualities.

Treatment

People with personality disorders rarely seek treatment on their own and are often mandated into treatment. They may voluntarily seek help once their behavior has caused severe problems: in relationships or jobs, or when suffering from another mental disorder such as depression or anxiety disorder, or when their drug use disorder is severe. Personality disorders are generally difficult to treat, but medications (e.g., antidepressants, mood stabilizers, antianxiety agents), counseling, and 12-step programs can help many people.

CHAPTER 12

Medications for Enhanced Treatment of Chemical Dependence

with Mark Evan Goldman, PhD

PATIENTS' OVERVIEW

Today's treatment of chemically dependent patients involves inpatient, residential (including intensive and halfway house), and outpatient treatment. These consist mainly of "talk therapy" and (in general) behavioral modification methods, including 12-step-based programs. The use of medications to enhance these programs and treatments is relatively new; yet medications (similarly to the use of medications in the treatment of clinical depression) can be a beneficial enhancement to the total outcome of the patient. While the medications discussed in this chapter are not "magic bullets," they are nevertheless extremely helpful for some patients. They are indeed the forerunners of medications that might eventually "cure" this disease.

Treatment for patients with a drug use disorder (either abuse or dependence) takes place in several venues. Because medical, dental, nursing, and pharmacy students receive very little training in addiction medicine, the hospital or medical center is not usually one of those venues. More often, the venue is the counselor's office or an inpatient or outpatient facility.

In a counselor's office (the office of a mental health worker, psychologist, social worker, or family therapist), diagnosis of drug abuse or chemical dependence is not always performed; therefore, the counselor uses methods simply to help a patient resolve drinking or drugging problems. There is great attention placed on the cause of the drug problem, often a discussion of past and current personal and family issues, and an attempt to "resolve" the causes of the drug issues in the individual.

Many drug counselors work in inpatient, residential, and outpatient treatment centers, and there the same individual counseling methods are used, but with supportive measures such as educational lectures, good nutrition, and recreation. Sometimes more evidence-based methods are used, including 12-step facilitation (orientation to the workings and successes of 12-step work), and even medications.

There are around 13,000 treatment centers in the United States, ranging from small facilities with only an administrator and counselors to larger facilities attached to hospitals and with a more diverse staff.

Inpatient Facilities

Inpatient facilities are places where patients are assessed, admitted, detoxed, and housed for 30 to 90 days. These tend to be costly because there are physicians, nurses, and other professional staff, just as in a medical center (but on a smaller scale). Many of these facilities (centers) are nonprofit, but because insurance does not yet cover drug use disorder treatment, patients are usually required to pay the costs themselves. (In 2009, the U.S. Congress passed a parity bill to mandate insurance coverage for treatment of mental illness and drug use disorders, which will make such treatment affordable and accessible to a larger number of patients.) Today, treatment in an inpatient facility ranges from about $5,000 to $100,000 per month. The quality and success of an inpatient treatment center, however, is not related to the cost of treatment. Many inpatient facilities also have family programs to help patients' family members learn about the treatment process and how the patient will change during recovery.

Residential Facilities

These include intensive residential programs (14–45 days) with structured individual and group therapy, drug education, and therapeutic activities. Many programs also have a family treatment component in which family members spend 4–5 days in a residential stay and attend family sessions during the patient's residential stay. Halfway house programs (typically 90–180 days) are used to help the patient transition back into the community, and typically follow placement in an inpatient or residential program. In this setting, the patient resides in a community-based facility, attends 12-step meetings at the program and in the community, receives counseling from onsite staff, and may hold a job, until a transition back home.

Therapeutic communities (TCs) are drug-free longer-term residential programs (usually 9–18 months) that use a hierarchical treatment model with stages for increased levels of personal and social responsibility. The emphasis is on using peer influence through community and group process to help individuals recognize attitude and behavioral deficits, and on developing appropriate social norms that lead to more effective social skills. The main goals are individual change, personal responsibility, and growth by helping people change their thinking and lifestyles using a community of fellow patients. TCs place emphasis on patients being active and responsible "community members"; hence, members actively help manage the program and serve as appropriate role models for others. Many TCs also now provide adjunct services for detox, outpatient treatment, family education, vocational training, medical and health services, and aftercare.

Outpatient Facilities

Outpatient treatment is less expensive and the patient is able to work while being treated during the day, in the evening, or on weekends. Outpatient treatment programs can be run out of inpatient facilities, or can be free-standing, or can even be carried out in a patient's home. Outpatient drug treatment involves group and individual counseling sessions, offering education on how to reenter society after treatment, how to lead a successful drug-free life, and how to work the steps in a 12-step program. Outpatient treatment can range from less intensive treatment (such as once-a-week individual, group, or family sessions for 1–2 hours) up to intensive outpatient or intensive outpatient rehabilitation treatment (such as 2–4 hours per day, 4–5 days per week).

Individual family and group counseling methods used in inpatient, residential, and outpatient treatment will be described in detail in Chapters 13–16. Contemporary treatment is beginning to place more emphasis on two areas: (a) evidence-based methods (i.e., those that have been shown to be effective in research studies) and (b) longer-term treatment to overcome the chronic disease of chemical dependence ("addiction"). "Evidence-based" generally means that at least some studies of treatment methods have been carried out to show that they work. Thus, 12-step programs have been studied sufficiently to be given the label "evidence based." Counseling methods such as cognitive behavioral therapy (CBT), motivational enhancement therapy (MET), and motivational interviewing (MI) are evidence-based, more so for the treatment of drug abuse than for chemical dependence. Examples of "treatments" that are *not* evidence based for the treatment of drug use disorders are "spa treatment," "famous chef," "relaxing facility," or "best views of the ocean," which many treatment centers describe on their Web sites.

One of the most studied evidence-based treatment modalities is medication-enhanced therapy, involving new medications that can be used for detoxification or to enhance abstinence. Interestingly, inpatient, residential, and outpatient treatment centers have often been slow to use these, primarily because some treatment centers do not employ medical professionals. Some state alcohol and other drug oversight agencies do require nursing and medical staff for differing levels of care, some more than others. However, 20 to 30 years ago this was not the case. Even some facilities with physicians and nurses on-site do not use all the available medications, or do not use these as extensively as needed, choosing instead to focus on counseling and other "talk therapies" and 12-step programs. This is usually related to an overly strict philosophy of seeing medications as crutches and the fear that people will over-rely on medications and not work to make personal changes.

Medication Overview

Medications for the treatment of "addiction" (chemical dependence) are rather recent in the history of disease treatment. Beginning with the old disulfiram (Antabuse) and continuing today, such medications have the promise of enhancing the treatment outcome of present talk therapies, with the effect of long-term healing of the individual who has lost control of drug-taking behavior.

Detoxification (Detox) Methods

Before any treatment is begun to keep a person free of drugs, the person must be removed from all drugs to clear the mind and body in preparation for learning about the disease and how to overcome it. This process is called "detox." In some individuals and especially with certain drugs, detox can be a life-threatening process. With others, the process is mainly uncomfortable and those going through it need some type of support to be able to accept abstinence training in the center. In yet others, detox produces no or few symptoms and is much easier. Because it is not possible to predict the severity of withdrawal, even regarding drugs with potentially dangerous withdrawal, patients are often placed in a specialized care unit and watched for the progression of symptoms that may occur.

Alcohol and opioids are the most uncomfortable drugs from which to withdraw. Up to 30% of heavy drinking individuals can die without proper supervision. Thus, sedatives (e.g., Valium) and other drugs to depress central nervous system (CNS) activity are used to ward off DTs (delirium tremens), to the point where DTs are rarely seen anymore during withdrawal. This is because detox personnel can predict the withdrawal symptoms of long-term, heavy drinking with the greatest accuracy. Opioids cause a severe, although generally not life-threatening, withdrawal in many patients. The acute withdrawal phase lasts 12–24 hours, with a more prolonged phase lasting for up to 7 days. Medications that are used during withdrawal include clonidine (Catapres) to reduce uncomfortable autonomic symptoms of elevated blood pressure, sweating, cramping, and tremors. Sometimes a sedative is added to reduce anxiety and other discomfort. Some detox units use "ultra-rapid detox," where the patient is anesthetized during withdrawal induced with the opioid antagonist naltrexone. Thus withdrawal is carried out within 12 hours with little discomfort to the patient. (This is *not* a cure for opioid dependence, as some proprietors have claimed.)

Withdrawal from amphetamines and cocaine do not produce life-threatening seizures or other physical signs; rather, the main problems are sleepiness, depression, anhedonia (inability to experience pleasure), and drug craving. The detox associated with these drugs is much more prolonged and is usually carried out in specialized inpatient settings where counseling methods predominate, because there are as yet no medications to overcome the dependence ("addiction") to these medications.

Withdrawal from benzodiazepines is also not life-threatening, but is very prolonged. Generally, withdrawal of a short-acting drug is managed by substituting a long-acting drug for the patient's current drug. Then by slowly "tapering" the dose over time, the patient becomes drug-free.

Medications to Treat Opioid Dependence

These medications consist of opioid agonists (meaning they activate opioid receptors in the same manner as the drugs they are used against), unlike the earlier unsuccessful use of opioid antagonists that block the receptors. Opioid antagonists such as naltrexone, when used many years ago, proved to be ineffective because dependent patients who often wanted to get high would not take the drugs. Thus, the current opioid agonists mimic the drugs of abuse but can be used under control with an emphasis on eventually getting the dependent patient off the medication.

Methadone (Generic)

Methadone is an opioid agonist (activator of opioid receptors) used to treat pain and opioid dependence. Methadone is a substitute for other opioid drugs so it is a pharmacodynamic "replacement" therapy and often referred to as medication-assisted treatment. By slowly introducing increasing doses of methadone to the opioid-dependent person, potential respiratory depressant and sedative effects can be minimized. The differences between methadone and other opiates is that methadone is synthetic and was engineered to have a long half-life (duration in the blood) so that once-daily administration and medical regulation can be achieved. Such issues play a significant role in harm reduction strategies, where it is assumed that some people will use the opioid (e.g., heroin), and methadone can reduce the harm to the user and those affected by the user (such as needle partners).

L-alpha-acetylmethadol (LAAM) is another opioid agonist that was approved in the United States to be used concurrently with methadone. However, it is now of only historical significance, because it has a dangerous cardiac side effect (QT interval prolongation) and was removed from the market in 2003.

Buprenorphine

Buprenorphine (Buprenex) is a potent (25–40 times more than morphine), semisynthetic pain medication that acts as a partial agonist and antagonist of the μ-opioid receptor. It is also used in the management of opioid dependence, and its trade name for this use is Subutex. Most commonly, buprenorphine is administered via the sublingual route (under the tongue), as a transdermal patch, and by IV infusion via patient controlled analgesia (PCA) pump. A major reason for using the sublingual route is to avoid "first pass" metabolism (i.e., a large amount of degradation of the drug) by the liver. Because buprenorphine is metabolized by the liver, health care prescribers should check to determine if the patient is also taking other drugs that are metabolized by liver enzymes. Buprenorphine has the same adverse effects of other opioid medications (nausea, vomiting, drowsiness, itching, headache, orthostatic hypotension, and urinary retention).

By itself, buprenorphine is a highly addictive and abused recreational drug in Scandinavian countries, although it is highly regulated in the United States. In combination with other CNS depressants (especially benzodiazepines and alcohol), adverse effects are additive and, therefore, very dangerous. This medication has been approved in combination with naloxone to prevent abuse potential (Suboxone).

Medications to Treat Alcohol Dependence

In most people, alcohol is rapidly metabolized in two steps to acetaldehyde and then acetic acid, which is easily eliminated from the body. In certain populations (such as Asians and some Native American Indians), there is an alteration (allele) in the gene that forms acetaldehyde dehydrogenase, with a subsequent reduction in activity of the enzyme. For many members of these populations, if they consume alcohol, they will experience toxic symptoms (rapid heart beat, flushing, dizziness) related to high levels of acetaldehyde accumulation.

Disulfiram (Antabuse)

Disulfiram was the first drug approved to treat alcohol abuse and has been studied for over 50 years. This medication significantly slows down the enzyme called acetaldehyde dehydrogenase, allowing toxic levels of acetaldehyde to accumulate after a person consumes alcohol. Symptoms include flushing, difficulty in breathing, headache, tachycardia, hypotension, nausea, and vomiting. The upsides to disulfiram use are few side effects (if the person does not drink alcohol) and simple route of administration (oral). The downside is patient compliance with the medication. Thus the best success with this medication has been in the judicial system and mandated treatment (such as in repetitive cases of drinking while under the influence [DUI]). (This drug is felt to be better at reducing alcohol abuse than alcohol dependence.)

Naltrexone (ReVia, Depade)

In the past two decades, naltrexone has been shown to be effective in treating chronic alcohol dependence. The U.S. Food and Drug Administration (FDA) has approved naltrexone for this use. Many scientists and clinicians believe that naltrexone is an underutilized treatment for this disease. Naltrexone is speculated to block the normal endorphin-mediated mechanisms that stimulate dopamine reward pathways during alcohol intoxication. By blocking these reward mechanisms, the person may learn not to expect the rewarding effects of alcohol. Additional well-controlled human studies have demonstrated and verified that a subpopulation of genetically defined alcoholics may be more susceptible to the beneficial effects of naltrexone.

An extended release form of naltrexone (Vivitrol) is now available as a once-a-month intramuscular (injectable) formulation. In combination with psychosocial intervention, it produces improvements in the quality of life, specifically in mental health, social functioning, general health, and physical functioning.

Naltrexone is known as an abstinence-enhancing drug, as a relapse-blocking drug, and as an alcohol craving–reducing drug. It is not a magic bullet, killing the craving for alcohol instantly after being prescribed. Rather, it works in less than half of patients for whom it is prescribed, it has mainly been studied in alcohol-dependent patients, and it should only be given in conjunction with counseling or an abstinence-based program or therapy. It has few side effects.

Acamprosate (Campral)

Acamprosate is an FDA-approved drug for treating alcohol dependence and is hypothesized to be effective in blocking N-methyl-d-aspartate (NMDA) receptors and activating gamma-aminobutyric acid (GABA) receptors. In more than a dozen clinical studies acamprosate has been demonstrated to reduce both short-term and long-term relapse rates in alcoholic patients, when combined with psychosocial treatments. Like naltrexone, it has few side effects and should only be used in conjunction with an abstinence-based treatment program.

Ondansetron (Zofran)

Ondansetron is a serotonin receptor antagonist with uses in preventing nausea and vomiting in medical settings. More recently, ondansetron has been demonstrated to lower cravings for alcohol and drinks/day, especially in early-onset alcohol-dependent patients in combination with naltrexone and behavioral therapy. It has not yet been approved by the FDA for the treatment of alcohol dependence. Side effects are moderate.

Topiramate (Topamax)

Topiramate is an anticonvulsant drug with properties similar to those of phenytoin and carbamazepine in the treatment of epilepsy, although its mechanism of action may be different. Based upon its known anticonvulsant pharmacology and adverse event profile, topiramate was demonstrated to be useful in the treatment of alcohol dependence by affecting glutamate and GABA receptor activities. In addition, topiramate seems to reduce the craving for alcohol. It has not yet been approved by the FDA for the treatment of alcohol dependence. Side effects may limit its usefulness.

Medications to Treat Nicotine Dependence

Tobacco dependence ("smoking or nicotine addiction") is often closely associated with daily lifestyle events such as concentrating, consuming alcoholic and nonalcoholic beverages, and socializing. It is also a significant drug use disorder for 80%–90% of people entering treatment for alcohol and other drug dependence, as well as those with co-occurring disorders. It has been determined to be a major cause of morbidity (illness) and mortality (death) for people with drug use disorders who are in active use or in recovery. The cessation of use of tobacco products will significantly improve the health and life span of the user and people around them, and has been consistently linked to better alcohol dependence treatment outcomes.

Varenicline (Chantix)
Over the centuries, the cholinergic (acetylcholine) nervous system (including both muscarinic and nicotinic receptors) has appeared to play a role in numerous diseases as well as the treatment of these diseases. As molecular sciences have evolved, there has been a clear recognition of multiple and distinct nicotinic receptor subtypes; some investigators believe that a drug that has a very specific site of action will have fewer side effects than a drug that interacts with many (irrelevant) processes in the body.

An example of a highly specific system is the nicotinic receptor family where the receptor subtype defined as alpha4 beta2, or $\alpha4\ \beta2$, is involved in many of the actions of varenicline. Varenicline is a partial agonist of this receptor subtype. (Thus, the drug affects the same receptor as nicotine, but in a less detrimental way.) Varenicline is approved by the U.S. FDA for treating tobacco dependence, and because it is eliminated about 93% unchanged in the kidneys, it has no known drug-to-drug interactions. Varenicline reduces the craving for tobacco products and reduces the pleasurable effects of tobacco use and, thus, reduces the need for tobacco products. The most common adverse effect is nausea, but insomnia and vivid dreams have also been reported. It is contraindicated for those with kidney disease. Because of a small increase in depression and suicide as well as other psychiatric events while using varenicline, the U.S. FDA has issued a "black box" warning for the use of this medication; however, nicotine withdrawal alone can also result in depression and suicidal ideation in some people. Nevertheless, the beneficial effects of varenicline are much greater than its side effects, and it is considered the most effective tobacco treatment medication. In fact, a recent study in the United Kingdom of 58,000 people using nicotine replacement medications, and of which 11,000 used varenicline, showed little risk of suicidal ideation.

Bupropion (Zyban)
Bupropion is a sustained release product, initially marketed as an antidepressant (Wellbutrin), that selectively acts as a dopamine and norepinephrine reuptake blocker, and doesn't induce reinforcement or dependence in humans. It was discovered by accident when it prompted a reduction of tobacco use and decreased desire in smoking among many

depressed patients who used tobacco. Subsequently, it was found to be effective as a smoking cessation aid by reducing the severity of nicotine craving and withdrawal symptoms. Unlike many other products, bupropion is not associated with weight gain and, conversely, may cause a small weight loss with long-term use. Caution is necessary when bupropion is prescribed to people with a low seizure threshold (e.g., had recent alcohol or sedative withdrawal), history of seizure disorder, or anorexia nervosa, and with other minor precautions as described in patient education information. In a small study by the Mayo Clinic, it was shown to be effective when used with varenicline and has no contraindication when combined with other drugs. It also:

- doubles abstinence rates vs. placebo, and can be used along with nicotine replacement medications or varenicline;
- reduces nicotine withdrawal and cravings; the effect on smoking abstinence is independent of relieving depression;
- is known that short-term treatment with this medication can lead to weight loss;
- is effective when nicotine medication alone does not work and for people who experience depression when stopping tobacco use; and
- should be started one week before the "quit date."

With all antidepressants, the FDA requires a "black box" warning that advises stopping use if there are unusual or adverse changes in mood, behavior, or onset of suicidal ideation.

Nicotine Replacement Therapies (NRTs,Smoking Cessation Products)

NRTs are devices used to reduce physical withdrawal symptoms after cessation of tobacco use. The devices produce a constant level of nicotine and are used to gradually reduce the levels of nicotine while the person is receiving counseling and other supportive therapies, including lifestyle changes. The goal is to slowly reduce the nicotine amount in the body while eliminating tobacco consumption. The most frequent cause of poor results is due to poor patient adherence (noncompliance), not using sufficient amounts to stop withdrawal symptoms, or using the medications incorrectly.

Nicotine Patch

The nicotine patch is an over-the-counter controlled release device that allows nicotine to enter the blood through the skin in a constant manner. It is often referred to as a nicotine withdrawal controller medication. While the effectiveness of the device varies among individuals, the American Cancer Society recommends the use of patches to decrease the severity of physical withdrawal symptoms. By delivering a constant low dose of nicotine and reducing the dose over time, the patch is a successful method for reducing nicotine dependence. The patch method is most effective when combined with other treatment methods including prescription medications, social services (such as coaching), or CBT. If the patch causes insomnia or unpleasant dreams, it can be removed before sleep and replaced upon awakening. It can be combined with bupropion, as well as with nicotine gum, nicotine lozenge, nicotine spray, or nicotine inhaler to control "break-through" symptoms and cravings.

Nicotine Gum

Nicotine gum is similar to the nicotine patch but is viewed as a rescue medication to employ on demand to reduce cravings and withdrawal symptoms. Nicotine is delivered to the body as with the patch method, by biting on the gum until a "peppery effect" is felt, and then storing it between the cheek and gum. While the nicotine patch is a once-daily treatment, nicotine gum can be chewed frequently (on a fixed schedule or as frequently as smoking) and can contribute to a lifestyle similar to smoking (but without the tars, carbon monoxide, and secondhand smoke). Potential minor adverse effects of this method include increased risk of birth defects in pregnant women, hiccups, dyspepsia, and sour mouth. People with dentures may find it harder to use. Nicotine gum is available over-the-counter.

Nicotine Lozenge

Nicotine lozenge is another U.S. FDA–approved approach as a rescue medication for delivering nicotine to the blood as a therapy. It is used on the same set schedule as nicotine gum. It is allowed to slowly absorb in the oral mucosa. The lozenge provides about 20%–25% more nicotine than does the nicotine gum and may sometimes provide more relief from cravings and the desire to use tobacco. The risks are the same as for nicotine gum. It is approved for sale over-the-counter.

Nicotine Spray

Nicotine spray is another rescue medication for strong cravings and withdrawal relief. It is used similarly to any standard nasal spray at 8–40 doses/day. The recommended duration of use is 3–6 months. Because it poses some risk of dependence, it is available by prescription only. Its primary side effect is nasal irritation, and it also has some pregnancy risk. It is most effective for highly dependent smokers (i.e., two or more packs per day, and those with serious mental health disorders who are smoking). It provides rapid absorption and fast symptom relief as compared to other nicotine medications, and can be used in conjunction with patch, gum, or lozenge, and with bupropion. Some patients with schizophrenia report a preference for this form, due to its rapid onset of effect and symptom relief.

Nicotine Inhaler

The name "nicotine inhaler" is a misnomer. It is actually an oral puffer and is used as a rescue medication. Nicotine is not inhaled into the lungs; rather, it is "puffed" into the mouth and absorbed through the oral mucosa. It can be used in conjunction with patch, gum, or lozenge, and with bupropion. The best results are achieved with scheduled and frequent puffing. Its primary side effects are irritation of mouth and throat, coughing, and rhinitis (nasal irritation). It is prescription-only and precautions for use are the same as with the nicotine spray.

With all of the above medications to treat opioid, alcohol, and nicotine dependence, there are some overall considerations. First, none of them is a magic bullet that will easily stop the use of an abused drug. They must be used with counseling or abstinence-based therapy for best results. Second, they will not work for everyone who takes them. Nevertheless, they have been shown to help save the lives of many chemically dependent people. Because the potential market for these drugs has been perceived by pharmaceutical companies as being limited, it has been difficult to develop an interest in drug development in this area by pharmaceutical companies. Hopefully this will change in the future through a clearer understanding of the science of chemical dependence.

CHAPTER 13

Principles of Individual Therapy

with Peter J. Pociluyko, MA, CASAC, CCS

PATIENTS' OVERVIEW

Individual therapy is the domain of the single-practice counselor, as well as a component of inpatient and outpatient treatment. Individual clinicians vary in their experience, training, and personal characteristics (empathy, patience, charisma), and all of these factors help determine how well a patient* with a drug use disorder can be helped. It is useful for students and clinicians to have a foundation for principles of individual therapy. In many cases, these principles apply to group therapy as well.

Abstinence is the nonuse of alcohol and psychoactive drugs. Sobriety is often thought to be the same as abstinence, but technically it means, "not being under the influence of a drug" and in Alcoholics Anonymous (AA) it implies having a clear and open mind. Thus most clin-

---

*A *terminology note:* Although most counselors call individuals with drug use disorders *clients,* we prefer to use the medical term *patients* because drugs cause important physical and mental problems that need treatment. (We are not talking about "bank clients" or "clients of insurance companies" here). Also, counselors working in this field have been labeled with many titles: "drug counselors," "drug abuse counselors," "substance abuse counselors," "addiction counselors," or "chemical dependency counselors," depending on state regulations and association preferences. In this book we prefer to use the term *clinicians* for these professionals, realizing that many clinicians are "counselors."

icians think of sobriety as a step beyond abstinence and as being involved in recovery. The Betty Ford Institute (2007) defines *recovery* as follows: "Recovery from chemical dependence is a voluntarily maintained lifestyle characterized by sobriety, personal health, and citizenship." (See Chapter 18 for details.) Recovery is generally viewed as an ongoing process that includes new learning, self-awareness, change in behavior and personal faults, and new self-identity—in other words, *change*.

The discussions in this chapter and the next chapters usually do not discuss "drug abusers" or "chemically dependent" patients, unless otherwise noted. Both of the above conditions have been loosely called "addiction," but newer practice tends to label people who have these conditions as "patients with a drug use disorder." The differentiation between drug abusers or chemically dependent patients is mainly scientific and is not always followed in clinical practice. However, as discussed in Chapter 1, the differentiation is critical in diagnosing who has a brain disease and who does not, when looking at treatment populations of problem drinkers and drug over-users.

Individual and group therapies help all types of patients, regardless of their label. However, previous chapters have indicated that drug use disorders with various severities are seen in practice, and we assume that therapies work best for those patients who do not have a severe disorder or disease.

What Is Drug Counseling?

Drug counseling is a specialized counseling profession based on national certification standards and is used to address the impact of drug processes on the individual, the family, and the community. The counseling process works to help patients identify and resolve drug use–related issues: family issues, relationship issues, employment issues, health issues, legal issues, and co-occurring issues. Techniques of various types are used to help patients and family members with specific outcomes. The primary goal of individual counseling is helping patients develop and maintain abstinence and resolve drug use–related problems. While it originated from Alcoholics Anonymous (AA) 12-step work, professional drug counseling is not 12-step work. Drug counseling requires professional training and clinical supervision, uses a code of ethics and clinical standards of care, and (when possible) incorporates scientifically based methods. Many drug counselors are in recovery and enjoy working in the field because they want to "give back" in return for their sobriety. They also have a unique connection with their patients. However, it is not necessary to be in recovery to be an excellent drug counselor.

Assessment—Using an Historical and Present Focus

Nearly all drug treatment follows a medical approach requiring a patient history before beginning treatment. A history is used to make a diagnosis based on measurable signs, key symptoms reported by the patient, and the severity and progression of the disease. A correct diagnosis can help lead to proper treatment by determining when detoxification, counseling, or medication is required. However, simply knowing the history of a drug use or co-occurring mental disorder does not necessarily support change. In fact, a focus on the past leads many patients to explain away problems and to explain why change cannot or should not occur. People with drug use and mental health disorders also selectively recall the past, leave out key details, and often reinvent their recall of events. Short of having a videotape of what the person actually did and said, it becomes a "he said/she said" impasse.

This does not make the past unimportant. For example, discussions of past mistakes and failures can be helpful to discover "lessons learned." Past successes can be used to plan ahead and look forward. Furthermore, once patients are abstinent and have some steady recovery, past exploration of interpersonal conflict, grief and loss, or trauma can sometimes be useful toward helping people remain abstinent.

Here are some methods for a counselor to become "patient informed." Simply ask:

- *What methods did you use to try to stop using? How long did it work and what happened?*
- *When you use drugs, what usually happens—positively? Negatively? What is different about each result?*
- *How is your present drug use different from 5 years ago? How is your use different from when you first began to use? What do friends or family say has changed about your use over this time?*
- *What are you feeling, thinking, and doing when you use? What are you feeling, thinking, and doing when you do not use? What is different between use and no use?*
- *After something negative (or positive) happens, what do you usually do? If you use drugs, what is the effect you obtain? What do friends or family say is the effect of your use?*
- *When do you tend to use more? When do you use less? When do you tend to not use at all? What is different about each time? How is this different from when you first began to use? What do friends or family say is different?*

A major area of inquiry includes social context: Who is around and what is the response by others when drug use occurs? For example:

- *Who is present when you use? Who is present when you use to excess or have problems? Who is present when you are not using?*
- *When you use drugs while with family and friends, what do they say or do? What do you do in response?*
- *When friends or family complain about your use, such as saying, "You use too much" or "You get angry," what do you do in response?*
- *If such people as your family, your employers, or your probation officer were here right now, what would they say about your use? About your behavior?*
- *When you are not using and have been abstinent, what are you doing differently compared to when you are using? What do others say and do when you are abstinent? How does that affect your abstinence?*

Most important, a counselor should not cast blame on the patient (or family) for the disorder or disease. Patients should be held accountable for any explanation or perception. The above questions also build rapport because of their respectful nature. Clinicians should actively seek the patients' perceptions, experiences, or insights about the problem. This method asks patients to consider the benefits, consequences, and reinforcing factors behind continued use, and elicits what solutions have been tried and what hasn't worked. It helps paint a picture of not only who are involved with the "problem of drug use," but helps understand how they are involved.

What Supports Change?

Change is inevitable and cannot be stopped, despite people trying to do the impossible and avoid change. To change and resolve any problem, change needs to be measurable. For example, some specific behavior, symptom, or effect to be changed must be identified. But solving a problem also requires a clear idea of what the solution will look like. The definition of the problem and a clear idea of the solution cannot be imposed by others. It must be something the person with the problem understands and accepts.

Change requires some form of positive feedback that ensures patients will follow the right path. This can be feedback from repetitive actions, from self-reflection, from the environment, from social interactions, or from others.

Small changes tend to trigger larger changes, just as a stone causes ripples in the water. For example, a change in a person's reactive emotional response will tend to affect thinking, behavior, and social interactions. A change in thinking tends to cause changes in emotional response, which often lead to behavior change. When a member of a social system makes a significant change in behavior (i.e., stops drinking), it will precipitate changes in family interactions and with peers.

How people talk about their problems, change, and solutions in turn affects their perceptions and thinking, and that influences the level of motivation to change or to not change. For example, when people focus on problems or use "problem talk," they talk about the past, how a problem started, why solutions did not work, and why they cannot change or should not change. That prevents thinking about the future, about the benefits or importance of change, or about the consequences of not changing. When people use "change talk," they focus on the present and the future and begin to talk about specific behaviors, emotion issues, or beliefs they need to change, as well as reasons for change.

The motivation to act and change (e.g., begin abstinence) is driven by internal factors (within the person) and influenced by external factors (such as health consequences, life events, family, friends, employer, court, or probation agent). Theoretical models indicate that importance plus confidence equals readiness or motivation to change. Furthermore, people must resolve their ambivalence about change; otherwise they will get stuck in a merry-go-round of wanting to change, yet staying the same.

Assuming the problem is well defined, the person must be willing to change, ready to change, and confident about change. However, confidence is more than a belief in oneself. Even the most confident person, ready and willing, may not succeed if it is not known what or how to act in order to succeed. Importance, willingness, and confidence can all be high, but the ability, skills, and knowledge needed to change are also important. One of the strongest programs to promote change is called "motivational interviewing" (MI) (to be discussed in the next chapter).

Resistance to Change

People tend to resist change, even when there is an overwhelming benefit to the change.

Resistance can refer to "forces within the patient, family members, a treatment group, or among peers" that impede insight, self-reflection, and change. Resistance is also interpersonal and is observed as a "pushing back" against pressure to move in a specific direction that is imposed by others.

Despite being adaptable, humans are highly predictable and consistent in their behavior. The best predictor of future behavior is recent past behavior. Individual behavior usually follows a pattern and repeats itself over time. In fact, most interactions between family and friends are based upon largely automatic, unconscious, fixed patterns of inter-action—akin to a set of rules that must be followed in sequence. People like predictability and stability and often "get stuck" in established and familiar patterns of behavior, thinking, reacting, and relating.

Many behaviors that look like resistance may not be what they seem. For example, a person who is conflicted and ambivalent about change will waiver between making some effort and shifting to a *"I cannot do it"* or *"it won't work"* stance. A person who may want to change but is fear-ful of change may be reluctant and will appear resistant. A person who is "resigned to his fate" and feels defeated from many efforts to acquire or maintain abstinence may appear resistant. A patient may recognize the importance of making a change, yet does not act due to lack of con-fidence to succeed. A confident patient may appear resistant to change because the importance of change is low. A patient may feel that change is important and has the confidence, but lacks the important skills and abilities to act.

Resistance to abstinence and to change in the direction of recovery is complex; it comes in a variety of forms and usually has multiple support-ing factors. Resistance to stopping drug use can result from neurobio-logical changes in the brain that override rational and conscious choice while unconsciously driving a need to use. Resistance can also be driven by ego-defenses used to avoid painful memories or feelings. Resistance can also be a conscious and deliberate choice. Or there might be resis-tance based on fear that change would eliminate positive reinforcement (positive effects) from drug use and other behaviors. Stopping use tends to produce negative consequences (for example, withdrawal discomfort), so people maintain use or return to use to avoid these effects (negative reinforcement) and resist change to avoid consequences.

Resistance can also be caused by and increased by a counselor's behav-ior, especially when patients are not ready to change and not ready to use an intervention, or if everyone is "not on the same page." It is tempting to want to "be helpful" by actively persuading patients about the problem's urgency and about the benefits of change. However, these tactics more often increase resistance and diminish the likelihood of change. Many times clinicians, in their desire to see results, encourage, coerce, cajole, persuade, and confront patients to implement changes they are not yet ready to make. Clinicians may assume the patient is ready to move for-ward, but have not recognized unresolved patient ambivalence, and then are confused and annoyed that the patient did not follow through on a given task. In response to perceived resistance, clinicians try "more of the same" and become more persuasive, confrontational, and argumentative—yet only increase the patient's resistance. Strong or heavy confrontation about the need to change often increases people's defenses and unwillingness to change.

Giving people directives or advice, insisting on certain action steps, and not taking time to work collaboratively increases resistance. When clinicians try to "push their agenda for change" or prescribe how the change should occur, people resist.

As discussed in later sections, while confrontation is sometimes needed at specific times, resistance is better addressed by using a nonconfrontational method, sidestepping the arguments, and using patient-centered approaches that focus on what the patient is willing and motivated to do.

CHAPTER 14

Individual Therapies for Drug Use Disorders

with Peter J. Pociluyko, MA, CASAC, CCS

PATIENTS' OVERVIEW

Having learned the principles of individual therapy, clinicians, students, and patients can now begin to understand the different types of counseling methods. All of these are important, but there are as yet few studies of their effectiveness. We know people get better with these therapies. Less well understood are the types of therapies that match certain situations and individuals. Knowing the different methods allows a better choice of method for the particular problem being addressed.

Being patient-informed, clinicians should focus on what people want to change or accomplish and not what the clinician wants them to change. This avoids jumping to conclusions about how to solve a problem, without agreement and collaboration with the patient. Solution focused therapy (SFT) and motivational interviewing (MI) are especially patient-informed methods.

SFT is a collaborative, patient-centered approach that uses techniques to support change and resolution of well-defined problems. The goal is to help patients change their perspective, thinking, experience, and behavior and to resolve a problem in ways they find acceptable. This approach presumes patients have the ability and capacity to change using their own strengths, resources, and assets. However, they need guidance in defining the problem and applying solutions that support change.

MI is a collaborative, patient-centered, and directive method for building motivation to change. It builds discrepancy between a patient's stated goals and their present condition (problem state), while helping patients explore and resolve their ambivalence about change. Using a "directive" does not mean the clinician tells patients what they should do or tries to convince or persuade them to take a specific action. "Directive" means being an active partner who helps the patient verbalize problems requiring change, and reasons for why they should change. This approach supports patient autonomy and acknowledges that it is ultimately a patient's decision to change.

While there are many types of reflection used for different reasons, MI refers to three basic types of reflection. A *simple* reflection repeats and reflects the patient's statement with little or no elaboration. This acknowledges and validates what was said. A *double-sided* or *two-sided* reflection captures all sides of a patient's ambivalence. It acknowledges what the patient states, then uses "and, in addition, or also," to express the other side of the ambivalence. An *amplified* reflection reflects back what the person said and enhances any underlying but not overtly stated meaning, or slightly exaggerates what was said. It will often prompt patients to recognize and elicit the other side of their ambivalence.

Reflecting what a person stated (content) and the person's feelings (process) is common, and is not the only focus of a reflection. Here are the important forms of reflection to use:

- Reflection of content: *You did not use coke last week.*
- Reflection of feelings: *You felt happy or sad.*
- Reflection of thinking, imagery, or behavior: *So in your mind you said, "This is a bad idea." In your view, this did not look good. So when this occurred you reacted by doing the following. . . .*
- Reflection of perceptions, values, or beliefs: *You believe that your family is the most important part of your life.*
- Reflection of meaning: *You sound like you were angry that nobody called you back, after making that effort. It also sounds like you felt really disappointed and hurt.*

Not all patients respond effectively to reflections or questions about their emotions, and will instead respond to reflections of perceptions, thinking, mental imagery, and behavior. Some respond better to what they assume other people think, feel, do, or perceive. Asking certain patients about emotions, especially early in treatment, will make them more agitated, anxious, guarded, or confused. This is especially true with people who appear chronically hostile, who are hypervigilant (paranoid), or who are dealing with extreme feelings of guilt. Frequent reflection of emotions and feelings with a person who is hostile, suspicious, depressed, guilty, or hopeless tends to prompt feeling more of these same emotions.

Developing Rapport With a Patient

Active listening and empathy can be used to establish rapport. Empathy, however, is much more than simply identifying the other person's feelings and "reflecting" an understanding of their emotions. Empathy as explained by Carl Rogers—the originator of patient-centered therapy—concerns the understanding of another person's internal frame of reference, including thoughts, beliefs, feelings, perceptions, values, and behavior. After that, the clinician should be able to communicate to the patient an understanding of the internal frame of reference.

A key method used to demonstrate understanding and empathy is reflective listening and summarization. Reflective listening involves a process of periodically and briefly restating what the patient stated, felt, thought, or meant. This validates that the patient was heard and understood. When patients perceive being misunderstood, most will clarify the other's misunderstanding. Summarizing is also reflective listening used in a longer form: *I'd like to summarize what I understand so far. We have discussed . . . Does that capture the key points? Did I miss anything?*

Along with listening and empathy, the clinician affirms the positive, such as the patient's strengths, skills, knowledge, effort, and willingness to come to sessions. Affirmations must be genuine: *I appreciate your coming to the session today and for being on time. Despite many efforts to stop using, I am impressed that you have not given up becoming abstinent.*

The counselor also needs to ask questions to elicit specific information. SFT and MI use a respectful approach and recommend "asking permission" before asking questions and before offering information. This reduces the risk of a person feeling interrogated or of a counselor pushing a personal agenda. This also allows the patient to control being asked too many questions or feeling pressured to accept or learn new information: *I need to ask some questions about what brought you here today. Is that OK?* (Patient says, *That is fine.*) *OK, if I ask too many questions or seem confusing, please tell me.* Questions should be posed one at a time and the person allowed to fully respond before a reply is given.

People should not be asked two or three questions all at once or in rapid order. It is also important to use about two to three reflective or summary statements for each question asked.

Two additional strategies used in SFT and MI are useful. First, these methods use open questions to encourage full, meaningful answers about the patient's knowledge, perceptions, or feelings. Open questions help patients to more fully explain their thoughts and ambivalence, and to expose hints of desire to change. This approach balances asking questions with a much greater use of reflective listening and summarizing. Second, closed questions are used when asking permission, needing specific information, confirming understanding, or asking if a patient is willing to try a new direction or to take the next step forward in treatment.

Some clinicians ask about and reflect a person's perceptions, which might be more useful for developing rapport than reflecting feelings or asking about feelings. For example, *Can you tell me what brought you to this program?* The counselor then reflects the patient's content: *OK, the district court judge ordered you to treatment. What do you think was the judge's reasoning for doing that? What were the reasons for making that decision?*

Rapport is also increased when people use the same basic rules of social interaction. These include (a) how culturally appropriate it is to be apart from or near the person when standing or sitting, (b) an acceptable degree of eye contact, (c) approved gestures, and (d) the use of the same pace, tone, and volume of speech. To speak using similar wording and colloquial of language (assuming the meaning is the same for both parties) is also important.

Overcoming Ambivalence About Change

Regardless of method, an important step defined by MI is helping patients to resolve their ambivalence about change. Ambivalence takes the form of a conflict between two courses of action (e.g., using or not using) and assumes that each course of action will have benefits and costs. Many patients have never taken the time to identify, explore, or express the many confusing, contradictory, and unique elements of their internal conflict. For example, *If I stop using heroin, I will feel better about myself, but I will lose all my friends and feel unhappy, and I won't be able to enjoy making a deal to buy*. The clinician's task in this case is to facilitate expression of all sides of the patient's ambivalence, guiding the patient toward an acceptable resolution that can trigger change.

Strong, confrontational, or direct efforts to produce abstinence or any change is not effective at resolving ambivalence. Yet it is tempting for counselors to "jump in and help" by "pushing an agenda" and arguing that the patient must see the urgency of the problem, see the benefits of change, and make a commitment to change. That also usually results in reactance—it prompts the patient to move in the opposite direction and to become *more* resistant to change.

MI specifically makes the case that once ambivalence is resolved, it is the clinician's job to use strategies to elicit statements about change from the patient. It is not the clinician's job to suggest or impose reasons why the patient should change, or to confront the patient or argue why the patient should change. The approach can work by having the patient do most of the talking and to express the reasons and needs for change. If necessary, silence by the counselor is used to place the responsibility for discussion on the patient. When people resolve their ambivalence and begin to commit to making a change, specific methods are used to support the patient.

One method is using evocative questions to elicit change talk. For example, *What problems have occurred due to your drug use? If your drug use continues as it is now, what will it be like in 5 years? If you were to decide to stop using, what would be the advantages? If you decided to stop your drug use, what are the first steps you would take?*

When change talk themes emerge, the clinician asks for elaboration and specific examples: *Tell me more about that. When was the last time that happened? Give me an example. What encourages or increases your desire to do that?* When solution talk emerges, the clinician should ask for specifics: *So when this problem is solved, what will you have specifically done and what will things look like?*

Another MI technique (also used by other therapies) is to ask decisional balance questions to explore all four quadrants of drug use: (a) the advantages of using (good things about using), (b) the disadvantages of using (not so good things about using), (c) the consequences of stopping use (not so good things about stopping), and (d) the advantages of stopping use (good things about stopping). This provides a balanced view of all sides of the patients' arguments for and against change and helps address ambivalence.

MI (as well as other therapies) uses a "look back" method by asking about a time before the current situation emerged. *How were things better in the past?* (Reflects patient response . . .) *So how have things changed since then?* (Reflects response . . .) *What things are different now?* This can be used with a "looking forward" approach: *How will things be in the future by not changing or by keeping the status quo?* The counselor then shifts to asking how things would be if the patient made a change, and asks for specifics.

Like SFT, MI uses the "look forward" or "crystal ball" question, followed by reflective statements: *If you were totally successful in abstinence, recovery, change, and so on, and things are going well, what would be different? For example, what would be the first thing you would notice that was better? What would be the next thing? How would this affect your relationship with others? What would be different about your health and your recovery? How would your relationship with your family be different?*

SFT and MI use scaling questions about the importance and confidence in resolving a problem. Here is an importance question: *On a scale from zero to ten, where zero is low and ten is high, how important is it for you to stop using heroin, alcohol, and so on?* Instead of following up by how to increase the scale (which pushes an agenda of change), the clinician follows up with something like, *Why are you at a score of two, three, and so on, and not at zero? What keeps your score from going lower than it is?* Here is a confidence question: *On a scale of zero to ten, if you decided to stop using drugs, how confident are you that you could stop and remain abstinent?* When a patient begins to consider change, the counselor shifts by asking about how high the importance needs to be in order for a change to occur: *How high on this scale would this have to be to make you decide to change? What would be the difference between the score of where you are now and that score?*

MI recommends that clinicians avoid giving advice and instead offer information, and to first ask for the patient's permission. Advice giving is, I *think you should do the following . . .* or, *If I were you I would do the following. . . .* Many clinicians erroneously give advice or directives and expect patients to follow it. Offering information is different: *There are several reasons why the effects of using heroin are reduced and why you feel the need to use more of the drug. Are you aware of why that occurs? (No) OK, would you be interested in knowing why?* Offering information requires determining what the patient wants to know, what the patient already knows, and then asking if the patient is interested in learning more information. After that, information is shared in small bites, not large chunks.

Both MI and SFT use reflection, summarization, and questions to find discrepancies between a person's current problem and desired state. This helps to surface conflicting issues and can lead to a resolution of ambivalence. When people are using change talk and solution talk, SFT takes this one step further and uses "exception questions" to identify when a problem such as drug use is less severe and what people are doing differently. This is a strategy to help people identify their own internal methods of support for recovery and change. The following examples illustrate this: *When is your drug use less severe or when do you not use at all? When is it at its worst? What was different on days when drinking or drug use was less severe or when you did not use? What did you do differently to make things less of a problem or less severe?*

A clinician can use "reframing" to relabel a negative behavior and give it some positive intention or purpose, for example, reframing a person as having a neurobiological illness instead of defining it as a lack of will, lack of morality, or being irresponsible. Reframing a relapse that has brought a patient back into treatment as "an opportunity to learn how to successfully recover" is another example. Redefining stubbornness as "determination" that could be used to support recovery can be helpful for some patients. Reframing can also be used to relabel a negative perspective, such as overuse of a behavior that is self-defeating: "caring too much, thereby preventing the person from growing up by learning from natural consequences." Patients need to hear their own words and meanings when provided with a reframing of a problem. Reframing a patient's description of a problem into a language that is understandable and acceptable to the patient will help promote change.

Helping Change Perceptions, Thinking, and Behavior
The effectiveness of cognitive therapy (CT) and cognitive behavioral therapy (CBT) for the treatment of drug use (tobacco, alcohol, cocaine, marijuana, opiates) and mental health disorders has been well documented. Many of the same skills and techniques used in SFT and MI are also used in CT and CBT, and all of these approaches can easily be blended and integrated.

Both CT and CBT assume that feelings and behaviors are primarily driven by a person's perceptions, thoughts, beliefs, and interpretations, and are not necessarily due to external causes, people, or situations. Accordingly, how people perceive and interpret events leads to certain emotional responses and behaviors. Research does show that people who routinely feel depressed also think in negative, self-defeating language and they act depressed, which reinforces their depressed mood. In other cases, depressed people have low levels of serotonin and other brain chemicals, which might cycle to produce different levels of depression (depression of unknown cause). Cognitive processes such as perceptions, beliefs, and assumptions about oneself and others actually underlie and drive much of our emotional experience. A person's emotions are likely to change after beliefs and thinking change.

According to CT and CBT, people may not be able to change their circumstances. However, they can change how they view or think about problems and therefore change how they feel and behave. CT and CBT also focus on behavior. For example, teaching patients to recognize situations in which they are most likely to use alcohol, tobacco, or other drugs, and to avoid these circumstances if possible, may lead to lower drug use. For patients who are actively working to change, providing practical problem-solving skills training helps to support a behavior change and thus results in higher abstinence rates. Patients also benefit from skills training that address physical, relationship, behavioral, and emotional areas. CT and CBT can also be used to examine how people behave and react in interpersonal situations, especially those where there are cues, prompts, or encouragement from others to use drugs.

CT and CBT both use a blend of cognitive and behavioral methods. The clinician observes, identifies, and helps the patient to look at thinking and feeling before use, what triggers the desire or behavior to use, and what occurs while using and after using. This helps to map out antecedents or triggers for feelings, thinking, and behavior that support drug use. The assumption is that addictive behavior is reinforced by positive results and is also supported by an attempt to reduce negative feelings or thinking. Because behavior is observable, it is the most effective method of assessing change in the patient. The old adage by many members of Alcoholics Anonymous (AA), "Bring your body and your mind will follow," recognizes that a change in behavior will lead to a change in thinking and emotions. When people begin to act differently, they begin to think and feel differently.

CT uses techniques of reflection, summarizing, affirmations, and open questions. It also uses "Socratic questions" to help people to uncover, identify, and then challenge rigid and often irrational beliefs that support emotional and interpersonal problems. Another cognitive approach is a psychoeducation process that raises awareness, provides new information, increases discrepancies and subtly challenges old ideas about drug use and symptoms, and increases an internal desire to change.

One major task for the clinician is to conduct a functional analysis, in which the counselor and patient collaboratively identify thoughts, feelings, and circumstances that occur before, during, and after the use of alcohol, tobacco, or other drugs. This perspective offers an understanding of the "function" or purpose behind the behavior, its impact not only on the individual, but on the person's social context. It also examines the benefits and consequences of using the drug. In addition, it determines the supporting factors and risks that are likely to lead to use. This method provides the patient with insight into cues and triggers for drug use and identifies coping difficulties. Behavioral interventions are based on an understanding of "what is the purpose and benefit" and "what is the outcome" of the behavior.

A second task for CT and CBT clinicians is to help the person learn or relearn better coping skills. The counselor helps the patient look at old behavior and practice using healthier skills and habits, while also challenging irrational thinking patterns with rational thinking. The main goal of CBT is helping the chemically dependent patient to change the thinking about drug use and to learn new ways to cope with the cues and triggers that led to drinking or drugging episodes in the past.

Skills training to change behavior and thinking requires significant practice, which is often given with "outside session homework." A patient might be asked to practice deep-breathing exercises or role-play how to act and talk differently in certain social situations. A person dealing with drug problems might practice ways to decline an alcoholic drink or a cigarette. Homework is vital to the success of CT and CBT. Patients must practice new, rational responses until they replace their previous, unhealthy responses. Homework also allows patients to try new skills and give feedback to the clinician on what works best for them.

Coerced and Mandated Treatment

Addiction treatment often uses coercion to pressure patients to enter treatment or suffer significant consequences. Coercion by the court, social services, or an employer can be effective in getting someone into treatment; however, it does not instill desire or motivation to change. Furthermore, the issues related to coercion need to be recognized by clinicians and openly addressed with patients in order to build a therapeutic relationship.

When a person voluntarily seeks treatment, the clinician assumes the role of the patient's agent and is expected to provide effective care and protect confidentiality. In contrast, when a patient is coerced into treatment, the clinician is in the role of a "dual agent." Along with the role of counselor, the clinician is also an extension of the court, the parole board, employer, or the social service department that is mandating change in the drug user. It is therefore important to openly discuss this dual-agent role with the patient. Clinicians must be candid with their coerced patients about what can and cannot be shared with others. They need to tell the patients that what they discuss in therapy may sometimes be revealed to the mandating party, and that could have an impact on decisions about the patient.

It is important to recognize that collateral agencies (probation agents, social services, employers, and courts) often want the clinician to act on their behalf and may expect the program to compel the patient to comply with required changes. Patients in turn assume that clinicians agree with or favor the referring party's view and goals over their own views and goals. Understandably, many drug users respond to coercion by actively or passively resisting. However, if the clinician also emphasizes the use of power and coercion, and fails to rely on therapeutic skills to engage the patient and develop a working relationship, it merely leads to an "appearance of change" or compliance while in the program. This is exactly the opposite of the desired outcome.

A useful principle from AA and other 12-step fellowship groups is helpful to consider. AA established a principle that the only requirement for membership is a sincere desire to stop drinking, stop using drugs, and so on, but there is recognition that "if the body comes, the mind will follow." AA (and other 12-step fellowships) also apply a key concept that helping a person to become abstinent and recover is more about attraction (seeing the benefits of recovery through the positive effects on others) than promotion, pushing an agenda, or coercion. Using influence and attraction can appear less efficient than coercion and mandating treatment in lieu of punishment, yet it is more effective in developing rapport and engaging the person to examine the situation. The challenge for the clinician is how to focus on the best interests of the patient while also actively helping the patient to recognize the benefits of change, respecting the choice to remain the same, and considering the interests of the mandating party.

Common Therapeutic Mistakes

Two of the most common mistakes are (a) not working to help patients identify and resolve ambivalence and (b) pushing patients to make a change before they are ready to act. Some clinicians assume a take-charge approach, a "do-what-I- say" approach. They may insist they are "patient-centered," but in fact are not collaborative and mostly direct or "push their agenda" for what patients should do during treatment. Some will accuse patients of being in denial or being resistant, unless patients are in agreement with what the counselor already deems important. A respectful approach does not dismiss a patient's desires, concerns, interests, or strengths.

Clinicians also make the mistake of referring to certain patients by using the diagnosis or some pejorative label, often due to annoyance with a given patient, for example, *He is such a borderline! What do you expect from an alcoholic?* Or, *She is schizophrenic.* Every patient is more than a diagnosis. A diagnosis is a condition patients have, but it does not and should not be used to define them. How we think about people and the words we use to describe them has more negative effects than expected. Diagnoses of drug use or major mental health and personality disorders evoke negative and nonhelpful reactions from clinicians, who may view patients as hopeless, demanding, manipulative, and always seeking control of others. Patients pay attention to the subtle behavioral and verbal cues and some identify and internalize these unspoken beliefs and fulfill the expectations, that is, they become "treatment failures." What clinicians feel and think about patients is behaviorally communicated to patients, whether the clinician knows it or not. Many patients are keenly aware of the behavioral cues and signals from others, and will respond by not sharing information, canceling or missing appointments, demonstrating noncompliance with treatment, or other forms of resistance toward the counselor. Clinician behavioral messages influence the perceptions, feelings, and behavior of patients. While some patients always seem to defy expectations, many patients will tend to internalize a clinician's positive or negative expectations and act in accordance with them.

It is important to ask patients to define their "terminology" and assume a "not knowing" posture. If patients use street language or a local expression, do not assume you know what that means. Ask, *When you use that term, what does it mean for you? When you say, "He has an attitude," how do you know this? What does he or she do that tells you this is true?*

Aggressive, direct confrontation to defeat the patient—as if the patient is an opponent—is a mistake. This also undermines any effort to develop and maintain a therapeutic relationship. Use of strong confrontation can be related to the clinician's self-esteem being dependent on the patient's compliance and success. Thus, when the patient fails to comply, the clinician gets disappointed and then angry. Hardened or treatment resistant patients who are heavily confronted tend to become even more resolved to resist and "play the game" or simply abandon treatment. Strong confrontation is especially contraindicated with acutely ill psychiatric patients and people with low ego strength.

Many clinicians trained in addiction therapy, due to their experiences of personal recovery, readily share this personal information with patients. The intent is assumed to rapidly build rapport with the patient; however, there are many other skills and abilities needed to develop rapport and trust. One problem is overidentification with the patient (or with the spouse, partner, or children) and is often due to confusing professional and personal roles, leading to premature personal revelations that are countertherapeutic. Premature self-revelations often create the impression that the counselors need to share "their story" and those are more important than the patients' stories. These disclosures also clearly signal that the counselors' agendas and goals for the patients are abstinence and recovery. Many programs also have a mix of recovering and nonrecovering treatment staff, and such revelations can readily lead patients to assume that "recovering staff are better" and it can support a rift or a split among recovering and nonrecovering staff. Self-disclosure can be a very effective tool, when given at the right time, for the right reason, when the patient is most ready to use it, and when it is not the main tool for developing rapport.

CHAPTER 15

Principles of Group Therapy

with Peter J. Pociluyko, MA, CASAC, CCS

PATIENTS' OVERVIEW

Group therapy is so important as a primary treatment for drug use disorders that two chapters are devoted to it. For students and clinicians without a psychology background, this "principles" chapter will be informative. For patients who wonder about the effectiveness of this therapy, the general principles will serve to persuade them that the therapies not only work, but they can be lifesaving for patients in trouble with the overuse of drugs.

Joseph Pratt, a physician in Boston who treated patients with tuberculosis, used the first formal groups for helping people with medical disorders in 1905. Pratt found that when he organized regular groups of patients to meet and learn about their illnesses and to discuss common concerns, their recovery rates increased remarkably compared to those who had little or no social support. It became evident that social dynamics not only affect behavior and emotions, but also physiological processes.

From the 1920s to the1940s, American psychiatrist Harry Stack Sullivan developed the interpersonal theory of psychiatry, which became the foundation for most modern group therapy methods. Sullivan (1953) explained that the need to be connected with other people is basic, and people actively seek approval and avoid disapproval from important people in their lives. He concluded that one's sense of self-esteem and self-concept are highly dependent upon interactions with important people. Sullivan also noted that people with mental disorders interact with others using highly distorted perceptions. These interpersonal distortions are self-perpetuating and lead to self-fulfilling prophecies. Also, people relate to others based upon how they expect to be treated. In addition, people seek out others with similar interests, thoughts, and perceptions that help to support their own interpersonal distortions (a useful example is the alcohol-dependent person who says, "I don't have a drinking problem. Everyone I know drinks just like me."). Likewise, a person's distorted perceptions and related issues of self-esteem, behavior, beliefs, and emotional reactions can be modified by consensual feedback from a group of people whose perceptions the person trusts and values.

Sullivan (1953) concluded that there is an interplay among how pople think and feel about themselves, how they behave toward others, and how others think, feel, and behave in response. The research from the 1970s on self-perception theory is also relative to this issue. What we say (both aloud and internally) informs our beliefs and attitudes, and that in turn leads to conclusions about what we believe to be truth. This belief affects how we behave, and how we behave informs the strength of our convictions. This leads to another conclusion: If you say certain things about yourself or about others, you will come to believe that what you say is true (even if it is not), and you will act according to your beliefs.

The value of using groups for treating drug use and mental health disorders has been widely accepted for decades. Group therapy provides group cohesiveness, sharing of information, and identification with others with similar conditions. In addition, it instills hope, which is vital for recovery. It provides insight into one's behavior and how it affects others, and it allows reenactment or recapitulation of members' family interactions within the group. These are considered the most important factors in the treatment of the chemically dependent and patients with co-occurring disorders.

While economical, groups cannot or should not summarily replace individual therapy. Regular individual sessions are often vital to help the patient discuss individual progress and certain concerns, and to guide patients on how to discuss relevant issues within the group.

Planning a Group
Groups are an efficient and effective method for providing help, assuming sound planning and patient preparation. Planning a new group or

re-creating an existing group takes time, and poor planning will lead to inappropriate group members, higher patient turnover, chronic group conflict, and lower patient outcomes.

Basic group planning includes deciding on who is an appropriate candidate. How will candidates be prepared for the group? Who selects the group members? What are the selection criteria? What is the role and task of the group leader? How will the group be structured: open-ended or closed? Is the group open to new members being added at any time? And what are the desired outcomes?

Any therapeutic group requires a definition of its purpose, task, and goals. The goals are the global, long-term outcomes for the group members. The purpose is the reason why the group is meeting and the immediate or short-term goal. The task includes the steps taken by group members to achieve their goals. When any of these items are not clear, it is a primary cause for confusion within the group by members and the group leader(s). Furthermore, boundaries or "group rules" must be developed and explained to each member.

To illustrate, the purpose of an education-oriented group (hereafter called a psychoeducation group) is usually to learn about the effects of drugs and to identify how drug use causes problems. (In this case, the group leader must "study up" on the latest research on the effects of drugs so as not to provide inaccurate information.) The group goal may be to gain self-awareness about the negative effects of drugs and support a move toward reduction in use or complete abstinence. The group's task might be to meet weekly to discuss the personal effects of drug use. The purpose, task, goal, and boundaries should be reviewed from session to session, especially when new members are added. (Homework may include each group member studying an individual drug in preparation for reporting back to the group.)

Many decisions need to be made about the group meeting structure. How long will each session last? How long will a series of sessions run? A psychoeducation group may run for 1-hr, 1½-hr, or even 2-hr sessions, while a therapy group may meet for 1 hr or 1½ hr. The minimum and maximum size of the group also needs to be determined. Therapy groups work best when limited to 8–10 members. An educational group might have 10–20 members, and a community group session may be even larger.

Another issue is whether the group will be open or closed to new members. A disadvantage of open groups, especially in outpatient settings, is the loss of trust and reduced group cohesion that occurs every time a new member joins. As a result, existing members suddenly become less open to sharing and it takes time for trust to be reestablished. In residential and inpatient settings, open groups usually work well because the group members' interactions extend outside the session and because the group members interact constantly, as much as 24 hr a day. Closed groups are less often used, although they support greater group cohesiveness, are more focused on the therapeutic task, and work faster. But if members drop out, the group may lose its effectiveness. One strategy is a mixed-closed group where new members may enter or existing members may depart at specific times, such as every 6–12 weeks.

In a psychoeducation group the content to be covered and discussion methods are largely predetermined. Content relates to the group's task and consists of topics that the group is expected to discuss. The structure of an education group would likely involve an agenda for each session. The leader will manage an active discussion about some topic, asking questions of the group members, reflecting their examples, and drawing connections to the content. A semistructured group might have individuals each "report out" to the group and receive feedback. In contrast, an interactional therapy group usually does not set an agenda; rather, members discuss their behaviors, thinking, emotions, and problems related to their drug use disorder. Whereas the education group leader may be central and verbally active in most or all sessions, in a therapy group the leader might be active early in the sessions; as the group matures, the leader must shift to being a moderator and facilitator.

Many programs only allow a single group leader due to costs and need for having many staff generate service-based revenue. A co-led therapy group, especially with complex and disruptive patients, has many advantages including better group stability and lower dropout rates. Skilled coleaders who work well together can manage a larger group more effectively than a single leader. Coleaders also can better attend to group process more effectively and keep the group on task.

Content and Process in Group Treatment

To lead a group requires monitoring its content (what is said) and its process (the emotional tone and behavior of the group members). Content is the actual verbal or written message that people give and receive. Process includes individual behavior, behavior among subgroups, behavior between the leader and group, and the overall behavior of the group. It includes the group members' overall mood and what is openly stated in words and what is implied in tone and behavior. For example, a new member states, *My name is Michelle. I'm here because of an alcohol problem and because a judge ordered me to attend.* Her verbal statements are the content. However, communication occurs at multiple message levels, including body language, voice tone, volume, and pace of speech. It includes many mixed or contradictory messages. This is the process.

The content of a person's communication may be consistent or inconsistent with process. The inconsistency of content and process is especially common among those who are actively using drugs or alcohol, or are in early recovery, or who have co-occurring disorders, for example, "someone who talks the talk but does not walk the walk." Such patients may say they feel "fine" or "have no problems" yet appear sad, angry, or depressed. The less aware people are of their discrepancies, the more incongruent will be their content and process; the more incongruent, the less their degree of emotional and psychological health will be. Incongruence is a common thread in drug use and co-occurring disorders.

The biggest task of a group leader is monitoring the process of individuals, pairs, triads, and the overall interaction of the group. A leader may notice how a member introduces himself, who the person looks to when speaking, the mood, speaking tone, and volume. When watching the process among two or three people, a leader may see that one member poses questions or comments to another, yet is getting little response. The member continues to do so, despite not receiving any clear answers. The process might be that members shift from being open, expressive, and candid to a hesitant, reserved way of conversing, and avoid discussing anything too personal, especially after a new member joins or someone leaves the group.

Monitoring process requires attending to the emotional state of the group, including the group's "foreground" and "background." Foreground is the current mood of the group and varies depending on what is being discussed. Background is more important, reflecting the underlying mood of the group regardless of discussion. A group with strong trust will have candid or heated discussions that might threaten those in a new group, yet in the mature group, the background mood is one of trust and no one exits or gets frightened. After the heated discussion ends or a session begins, this group remains committed and cohesive. When groups are highly aware of their process, members take responsibility for their own feelings, thoughts, and behaviors and describe their feelings and thinking in the present tense. A less cohesive group will have a greater background of anxiety, distrust, and fear, as reflected by members avoiding confrontation or serious subjects and discussing safer subjects to create an appearance of normality and cohesiveness.

Basic Practices and Principles of Group Therapy
While originally designed for individual therapy, motivational interview-

ing (MI) principles and techniques readily apply to group treatment. It is important to use open questions, affirmations, reflection, and summarization; develop discrepancies; and roll with resistance. Patients should be urged to voice their own reasons about why drug use is a problem and why they need to change.

The key skill for managing and facilitating any group is to maintain a focus on the group as a whole and on the members' interpersonal process, while also addressing "issues" in the here and now. The most effective leaders balance concern for the well-being and contributions of individual group members and at the same time focus on the group's purpose, task, and members' responsibilities to share and resolve issues.

With therapy groups (and psychoeducation groups), group leaders often make the mistake of becoming caught up in listening to the past and to "problem talk," about such things as members' stories about why they cannot stop drinking, reasons why they started using, complaints about others, and their drug use rituals. It is easy to get "mesmerized" into listening to such stories and forget the group task and purpose. The task for the leader is to refocus the group into the present. One intervention might be to point out that the members are talking "as if these issues were resolved," rather than discussing their problems and difficult emotions as major concerns right now. This can be done by asking, *I noticed it is easier for you to talk about the past than the present. However, the past is not something you can change, so what is happening right now that is troublesome for you that you want to change?* When members reenact old feelings and behaviors, but talk about these in the past, another strategy is to get members to discuss emotions or behaviors from the past "that are happening now."

While exploration of emotions is important, it is not the only focus of change. Through activity of the group leader, the group should help the group members identify and challenge distorted beliefs about drug use, their belief in control over use, and the connection of thinking and strong emotions with relapse. This is most effectively done when group members challenge or question one another's irrational beliefs, irresponsibility, and lack of honesty that crop up during group discussions. The group leader may directly confront individual members about their thoughts or behavior, which is often not necessary and is usually counterproductive. Instead, indirect and subtle approaches, such as those used by MI, solution focused therapy (SFT), or cognitive therapy (CT) (to be discussed in Chapter 16) are more effective. These approaches do not directly feel threatening and provide a model for behavior in the group.

Some components of chemical dependence ("addictive") disease include poor judgment, as well as impulsive and irresponsible behavior. Hence, patients need to learn to contain their emotions and behavior, develop accountability, and delay gratification. For example, the group should always begin and end on time. Maintaining boundaries of acceptable behavior and encouraging members to do the same is an ongoing leadership task. Rather than being direct, it is best to ask longtime members to recite the rules, purpose, and task of the group, especially when new members are added or in a group that often goes off task. Group leaders need to avoid becoming complacent about the group boundaries or rules, such as failing to stick to established start and stop times. If the group is discussing a highly emotional issue during the last few minutes of the session, the leader should be aware of time limitations and announce when the group session is nearly over, and that the discussion can be continued at the next session. Sometimes leaders avoid setting this limit or fear that a curtailment of the discussion can be damaging. This action, however, violates good therapeutic practice, is poor modeling of limit setting, and signals an exception to members or topics.

Group leaders may need to be more active than usual in engaging members to discuss problems in a new group. As the group evolves, the leader should become less active, use indirect interventions, and shift to a monitoring role. That includes resisting the temptation to often respond directly, to self-disclose, or to pose questions that interrupt effective group process. Offering brief focused observations (one or two sentences) about how the group is behaving is more effective, followed by the leader redirecting the floor of discussion to the group. For example, in response to a quiet group and a group member posing a question to the leader, Sue is wondering why I think the group is so quiet. Instead of venturing a guess, it would help for people to talk about what they are feeling right now and what might be behind those feelings. Another strategy is to comment on the meaning of group behavior, which suggests covert expressions of concerns. Using the above example (when the group recently added new members): *When Sue asked me why the group is so quiet, I am wondering if people are feeling reluctant or afraid to share because we have some new group members?* Group anxiety or fears can be connected to drug use, such as asking, *When people feel this way, what are your usual ways of handling these feelings?*

Because some individual patient concerns need to be discussed outside the group, leaders must be careful about one-on-one meetings that appear to others as if one member is being favored. Individual sessions about the group or about topics to be discussed in the group can lead to members withholding feelings and thoughts from the group while sharing these in individual sessions. This creates the equivalent of a "secret" being withheld from the group. A useful technique to avoid such a pitfall is to ask that the member share with the group any private discussion related to the group or individual members.

Group Development Processes and Leader Tasks

The group level of functioning evolves and is dependent on how often the group meets, how long it meets over time, the level of trust and cohesion, and its stage of development. Having a conceptual model for understanding the developmental phases of groups and the typical behaviors that patients exhibit during each phase is useful for deciding the best interventions.

The stages of group development listed below often do not occur in short-term groups, such as four-to-eight-session psychoeducation groups. The development stages are more common in ongoing groups such as outpatient groups, day-treatment groups, recovery groups, and groups in intensive outpatient, residential, or inpatient settings.

While there are a number of models of group developmental stages, a commonly used approach is the Tuckman's five-stage model (below, published in 1965). This model suggests a linear sequence of discrete stages, but group development always has overlap and transition across stages; hence, there are no really discrete stages. Groups routinely return to earlier stages of development for various reasons.

While not specifically identified, a pre–group stage or a pre–forming stage is assumed, where individual patients meet with the leader about the group and develop an initial rapport.

1. Forming Stage

Groups mature through stages, and each involves different interpersonal dynamics and group tasks, requiring different group leader interventions. A new group enters a "forming stage" with members testing limits, some seeking to dominate the group and others attempting to form alliances with members or the leader. Often there is confusion about the role and task. Members may feel anxious, distrustful, tentative, and uncertain how to behave. Members will fear change and yet want to feel better (or stop feeling pressured to change by others) in the form of ambivalence. Members will tend to speak directly to the group leader or to group members they know or like, and will speak indirectly to other members by asking the leader what others think or feel, or believes others think or feel.

The leader has a number of tasks at this stage. It is important to frequently review the group boundaries, the purpose, and the task of the group in early sessions. In the very first session, introductions are needed, followed by asking members to discuss how they feel about being in a group, what they would like to "get out of it," and why they have come to the group. To help members develop appropriate norms (behaviors), people are asked to use "I" statements rather than "you" or "he/she" statements to describe behavior, and to focus on the "here and now." A new group will need to share common experiences and safe topics. Non-sharing can be allowed for one or two sessions, but then the leader should intervene to get the group on task. In subsequent groups, it helps to open with something like, *What is it you want to work on today?* or *Who would like to begin today?* with the leader then becoming silent. In ongoing groups the leader can also open with, *Is there anything left over from the last group meeting that people want to work on?*

2. Storming Stage

At some point, either gradually or suddenly, a developing group will shift to the "storming stage." This is demonstrated by overt conflict, little tolerance of differences, and individual members openly airing concerns or complaints. This is a critical stage of group development because the expression, recognition, and resolution of conflict are critical to group development to the next stage. Assuming the goals, purpose, task, and boundaries are clear, the conflict is a way to resist the group task, such as avoiding honest discussion about consequences of drug use.

Typical patterns are fight or flight, pairing, dependency, and fusion. Some will fight using verbal or nonverbal disagreement to stay off task. In response to group discord, some members may "flee" by becoming silent or changing the subject. Some members resist the group task by "pairing off" with others, that is, having "side conversations" to avoid discussing difficult topics and to avoid feeling their anxiety. The group may also go silent, resulting in the group leader working too hard by doing most the talking. Fusion occurs when members try to treat everyone as equal or the same (herd mentality) in an attempt to avoid defining individuality. This can lead to "group think," where members who disagree with this "we are all the same" mind-set are attacked and ostracized.

Common behaviors include frequent judgmental and absolute statements, such as, *I think you should do . . .* or *You always say stupid things like that.* Remarks about the need or usefulness of the group, including questions about what the group can do for members, can anger the leader. Sometimes there is an effort to "scapegoat" and blame some members who are seen as weak. A weak member often is one who is inadvertently being favored or is perceived as favored by the group leader. Emotional attacks also occur against members who polarize the group.

The natural response of a group leader is to jump into the fray and try to mediate or process what is happening when conflict occurs. Although counterintuitive, the first step is to not intercede, but to allow the conflict to unfold, comment on the group process, and then—at a later time—explore the issues and processes that transpired. Attacks directed toward a leader are usually not personal but a response to anxiety and resentment by the members. Acceptance of the conflict and requesting information will help members learn to tolerate and work through conflict. Self- monitoring is vital. A leader who is talking more than group members is preventing the group from addressing conflict, yet if the leader goes silent for too long, it is overly frustrating to group members. This must be balanced so that the leader does not become too active or inactive.

It is important to help the group adhere to acceptable norms of behvior. The focus should be on helping members use appropriate feedback when confronting others, that is, describe the behavior, indicate when it occurred, and explain how it made one feel. Also, attacks on others should not get "out of hand." Value judgments about others in response to group members should be avoided, especially those that verbally attack the leader or others.

A leader sets the tone and models the group when giving clear feedback to the group or to individuals, and when describing feelings about the group's behavior. Particularly helpful during the storming phase of the group, when members verbally attack the leader or a member, is to ask "seasoned members" to offer a comment about what they see occurring. This is an indirect way to refocus all the members to engage in discussion with one another, to support one another, and to resolve conflicts directly.

If a group leader is under verbal attack, the leader should not respond immediately to the members. Rather, the leader should listen to what is said, and then watch what the members do. Recognize that members in conflict often have accurate perceptions about a leader and specific members, so others can be asked about what they observe. If there is a co-leader, allow that person to comment on the group's emotional process.

The leader should deal with members' emotions by asking open questions about what people are feeling now, what people feared would happen when conflict erupted, what they most feared would happen, and what seemed to drive members' strongest emotions. This reduces fears by illustrating that controlled and open conflict is not dangerous. In addition, what members did, that is, who was attacked, who interceded, and who was silent, is important. When any "attacks" toward members are reported, members should be asked to describe the possible causes of this behavior.

It is important to be aware that some members may abruptly quit after an emotional session. It is important to discuss this possibility openly with the group at the end of a testy session. During periods of fusion and "group think," there may be indications that the group has moved into a "norming stage."

3. Norming Stage

After conflict has emerged, some groups will continue with conflict for a period and may revert back to a forming stage. Eventually the group will enter a "norming stage." It will then display some cohesion, greater trust, increased acceptance of members, and tolerance of quirky behavior. Members will now come to think of the group as its own. Some members will express that they feel safe in the group and will begin to express more personal thoughts, feelings, or concerns. They will more freely share things about themselves and about others that they find distasteful. If the group has been meeting for some time, members will tend to adopt appropriate roles, such as one member often telling the group when it is "off task." People will also assume roles and behaviors in the group that are consistent with how they normally act outside of the group. This is real "grist for the change mill." Members will begin to self-enforce boundaries such as remarking that a member tends to arrive late, or by stopping a member from changing the subject when a difficult issue is discussed. Group members may begin to question and challenge the leader(s). Group members will also begin to test out new roles and try using productive behaviors within the group. Because of the nearly euphoric feeling of trust and intimacy that can develop in this stage, there may be suppression of negative feelings toward others.

The leader's task includes continuing to promote open sharing of positive and negative observations and feelings among members. A leader should have reduced the frequency of interventions; if not, the group is allowing the leader to do the group's work. A key task of the leader is to watch for regression if a member leaves or is added, because the group may revert to a storming phase and make statements such as *Everything is terrible, the group is not working, this group is not helping me*. This is a stage when the leader can begin asking individual members to address specific issues, while simultaneously working with the group as a whole.

4. Performing Stage

When a sense of group cohesiveness continues over an extended time, some groups move to a high-level "performing stage." Now group members begin to think and function as "we." The group will be very focused on its task and equally focused on the importance of supporting individual members with candor. Members will balance praise and criticism—consistently giving useful feedback to one another. At this point the group norms and goals are very clear, with distributed leadership among various members. In this stage, members share feelings and observations openly, and demonstrate increased willingness to try new behaviors within and outside the group. Often some groups are actually "pseudoperforming" and have a sense of "group euphoria" where members hesitate to challenge a perceived "important" member, do not address serious issues in depth, and suppress negative emotions or concerns about others.

The leader's task includes ongoing observation while continuing to work with the group as a whole, yet to allow an increased focus on individual issues. It is important for the leader to watch for regression to earlier stages and to help the group move back to the performing stage if necessary.

5. Transforming/Mourning (Transition and Termination) Stage

The final stage is the "transforming/mourning stage," which includes adjourning or terminating and occurs during a time when members revert to older behaviors, emotions, and an earlier group stage. Transforming/ mourning occurs when members are planning to leave the group, when a member abruptly leaves the group, or when a new member joins. A process of mourning also occurs when the entire group is ending. For groups that are in the norming or performing stage, the departure of a member or termination of the group is felt as a loss. These feelings may not be recognized by the members and indirectly are reflected by frequent off-task conversations, avoiding discussion about the pending departure of a group member, or a sullen or quiet group.

Members will seek to avoid feelings of loss through a number of behaviors. Sometimes members suddenly raise new problems that appear to require the group's attention. If a group is ending all sessions, there is often a rise in absenteeism during the last few meetings. Members may also feel the need to say all the negative and positive things about members and the leader that they have kept hidden.

When someone is leaving a group, the members need to talk about how they feel regarding the loss of a group member. The leader should repeatedly call attention to the impending termination of the group member during the last few meetings. In a group that meets weekly, members should be asked to give at least 2 weeks' notice before actually leaving the group. In a group that meets daily or several times a week, there should also be a few days' notice. This allows the group time to process the anticipated loss and often triggers recall of past losses, including deaths, divorces, ended relationships, and the giving up of psychoactive drugs.

If someone leaves the group abruptly and without warning, it is important to process this for at least one or two sessions before moving ahead to other issues. Members should be asked about what they think happened, how they feel about that person and his or her absence, and whether they feel responsible for the member leaving. Members who appear to be avoiding discussion of termination through absenteeism, tardiness, or lack of participation should discuss their behavior and its causes with the group.

Knowing the above principles, it is now time to discuss specific group therapies and their effectiveness.

CHAPTER 16

Group Therapies for Drug Use Disorders

with Peter J. Pociluyko, MA, CASAC, CCS

PATIENTS' OVERVIEW

The best-known program for treatment of drug use disorders is the 12 steps, a mutual help method based on group interaction ("fellowships"). Not based on known psychological theories at the time it was started, it nevertheless is effective in helping many people stop using drugs and in helping them remain sober. Group therapies, as seen in the previous chapter, have developed from psychological theory and can be very effective. For clinicians, students, and patients, knowledge of mutual help groups and group therapy is important for understanding their mechanics and value. Too often, recovering counselors confuse fellowship groups with group therapy. People do not pay for mutual help support, and it should not be confused with or defined as group therapy.

Psychoeducation groups have an agenda with a few key points for each session (for example, eight sessions, each with an agenda). This may begin with the first session on a broad discussion of why people use psychoactive drugs, including the types of drugs used. In a later session, the topic may be "When Is Drug Use a Problem?" and other topics that seem relevant to the group. Agendas serve as guidelines for the main points to be covered in each session and may be repeated as a regular cycle. It is helpful to allow patients to attend the round of sessions more than once.

This is helpful with people who have co-occurring drug use and mental health disorders, or who have problems with cognition and memory. "Repetition is a good way to effectively learn something important."

Leading a psychoeducation group does not mean the leader should lecture or assume the role of an expert who gives advice or tells people "what to do and how to do it." Many clinicians have a deep reservoir of expertise, which should be shared in small amounts when appropriate. "Pushing an agenda," as in telling people what is good for them, what they should do, how they should act, and what to think, readily leads to not listening and to resistance. To avoid resistance, information is best offered using the spirit and principles of motivational interviewing (MI). Offering information is much different from giving advice or direction.

For example, notice the difference between *You need to stop drinking because it has caused you three DWIs. You need to stop drinking because it is harming your health,* and *Moderate drinking (equal to two drinks per day) rarely causes problems for people. Heavy drinking (defined as five or more drinks in 24 hours) consistently leads to legal, social, and health problems.* The first statements are advice-giving and very directive, whereas the second set of statements is simply offering information.

Here's another example. Notice the difference between *You need to stop smoking because it is bad for your health and if you don't stop, it will trigger a desire to use other drugs and cause you to relapse* and *Tobacco use causes many health problems. There are several studies that show that ongoing tobacco use increases the risk of relapse for people who are trying to remain abstinent from other drugs.* The first is directive and advice; the second is simply information.

When presenting information, it must be relevant and something the group is ready and open to learn about. If the group leader (counselor) presses the group to recognize a connection or offers unsolicited information, it turns into "giving advice," and that leads to resistance. It is better for a leader to provide information using a patient-centered approach, without arguing an agenda, preference, or bias. The leader should avoid using phrases such as "you need to," "you should," and "you must" when providing information. Instead, use a neutral, businesslike tone, and give information rather than saying what the patient should or should not do.

A useful method drawn from MI and applied to psychoeducation is the elicit-provide-elicit (EPE) method. This uses a cyclical process for gradually providing information in small chunks by using a neutral, straightforward style. It revolves around asking open questions, then asking permission to offer information, then providing a small amount of information, followed by more open questions as well as the use of reflective listening.

Step 1. The group leader asks members open questions (*elicits* information from group) to focus the scope of information, such as *I am sure this group has a fair amount of knowledge and experience, so let me ask what you would like to know more about regarding alcohol, opioids, cocaine, and other drugs* or What *do you already know about . . . ?*

Step 2. The leader asks permission to *provide* information to a specific individual or to the group, which is presented in a manageable chunk: *Would you like some information about . . . ?* or *Is it all right with you if I share information about what happens when . . . ?*

Step 3. The leader asks the group members for their reactions (*elicits* information from the group) to small chunks of information: *How does what I just shared fit with your own experience?* or *Given what you described earlier about yourselves and what I explained, what does this suggest (or mean) to you?* or *Would you like to know more about this or discuss this further?*

The leader's job is to facilitate and guide the group using principles and techniques from group therapy, MI, and solution-focused therapy (SFT). During the session, the facilitator thanks members for attending, asks them to freely pose questions and offer insights, explains the agenda, and begins the session. The leader gradually covers each key point by asking permission to share information or asking permission to ask questions. The leader also shares small bits of information at a time, then poses questions and elicits examples from the group members, while expressing empathy, reflecting, summarizing, and rolling with resistance. The leader also asks members to clarify and be accountable for "absolute" perceptions (such as *It always happens this way* or *The judge was out to get me*), builds discrepancies, poses open questions, and uses reflective statements to connect member statements with the agenda content.

Group Therapy/Group Counseling Interventions

Group interventions involve verbal and nonverbal responses by the group leader to help the group remain focused on its task, purpose, and goal. These responses can be in the form of questions or observations about behavior. An intervention refocuses the individual and group's attention to their process, refocuses the discussion to the here and now, and focuses responsibility for awareness and action on the members and the group. An intervention is also used to help the group and individual members to become aware of key emotions, thinking, behavior, and their impact. The type of intervention and how often to intervene will vary depending upon the group's stage of development. For example, after many minutes of a group talking about the past and future, the leader holds up a hand and says, *Let's stop for a moment. I notice that many members are talking about how great they will feel in the future and how awful things were in the past. Let's refocus to the present time. What awful feelings are people having right now? How are those feelings affecting your thinking and behavior? Later we can discuss what has gotten better.*

It is important to use open questions, affirmations, reflection, and summarizing, and to ask for examples. Within groups, it is important to begin by providing a summary of the last session, to present periodic summaries during the meeting, and to give an end-of-meeting summary.

The following questions provide a useful way to determine and evaluate the effectiveness of a group intervention:

- Does the leader need to make the intervention now or should time be allowed to see if the group corrects itself?

- What is the primary purpose of the intervention—to support the task, to support maintenance, or to support both?

- Does the intervention need to be focused on intrapsychic issues of a member, on the interpersonal process between members, or on the overall group process?

- Is the intervention focused on the past, the here and now, or on the future?

- Is the focus on content (verbal), internal and intrapsychic process, or interpersonal process?

- Is the focus on providing facts and information, exploring or clarifying feelings and emotions, or exploring or clarifying beliefs?

- Is the focus of the intervention to comment on leader-to-member interactions, member-to-member interactions, member-to-group interactions, or overall group interactions?

- Is the intervention appropriate to the group's stage of development?

- Is the responsibility for action placed back on the leader, the member, or the group?

- What was the effect of the intervention?

As noted in the above example, an effective group intervention shifts the focus either back to the individual member, to the member's interactions, or to the group process (this can be applied to psychoeducation groups as well). It also focuses on the here and now and places responsibility for action back on the individuals or the group as a whole. If group members talk about the past or why they kept using drugs, a leader might say, *Right now the group members appear reluctant to talk about current problems, although we have another half hour. What do people feel is happening right now to prevent our discussing current problems?* An individual member may avoid discussing troubled emotions by talking about the past or about plans, so the leader might say, *Bill, you have often spoken about how good things were in the past, and what you plan to do in the future. Can you talk with the group about how things are going for you right now?*

A common intervention is to remind the group of its task and point out when people are off task. An intervention about task is more common in the early stages of group development, but can also be required for mature groups sidetracked by changes or anticipated changes in the group's composition. A process-oriented group task is usually to discuss current problems, thoughts, and feelings in the here and now. However, if members begin talking about such topics as outside events and sports, a simple intervention by the leader would be: *The task of the group is to talk about issues in the here and now but the group is currently talking about the news. What are people feeling afraid to discuss, such that an outside event seems to be more important now?* Alternatively, with a more experienced group, the leader might say, *Is the group currently focused on its task?*

How often an intervention is needed and how complex the intervention is will vary depending on the group's stage of development. An intervention to a mature group is best delivered in the briefest of words. The leader should also go silent and observe what happens in response. A group in the forming stages may require more active and frequent interventions to keep the group on task. A leader's interventions and comments provide a model for the group on how they can intervene on their own. As groups mature and self-govern their behavior, the leader is more often silent and monitoring the process. Mature groups do inevitably regress to earlier stages and a less active leader will again need to become more involved.

The intervention focus should move away from attention on the individual to a focus on members and to the group process as a whole. An effective leader demonstrates the connections among all three areas. A leader comments on the group's effort to challenge a new member about his drug abuse, and connects the similarity of the new individual's behavior to that of a long-term member who often blames outside causes for poor recovery.

All groups, especially those in conflict, will assume opposing sides over an issue or over individual members, such as differences between cocaine addiction (or addicted members) and alcohol addiction (or addicted members). The leader needs to help the group identify and describe these polarities, by asking what is different about the "other opposing side." When such polarities are out in the open, the leader then asks members of each side to describe how the others are similar to them. The final question would be, *What has brought each of you to the present point?* or *Why is each of you attending this group?* The answers should come from the group and include responses such as *All members have a drug use disorder* or *All members have lost control of their use of drugs* or *All members have developed serious problems and cannot recover on their own* or *Drug use has severely affected all of their lives.* The final question is, *So what can you offer each other that could be helpful to recovery?*

Many group members assume their problem is so unique that no one could understand or have had a similar experience. A key leader technique is called *bridging* (some call this "linking"), whereby the emotions, concerns, or issues of one member are related to those expressed by another, either during the same session or from a prior session. For example, *George, your concern about how fights with your partner led to a return to opioid use on several occasions is very similar to something Sharon has described. She mentioned some time back how the conflict with her mother resulted in her getting so angry she would get drunk. What do you think or feel about this?*

When group members focus on "problem talk" (which leads to thinking in the past and does not lead to change or solutions), a leader can comment on their not focusing on the here and now, but on the past. Then the leader can ask the group to focus on what is currently a problem that the group needs to explore. When the group shows evidence of "change talk" or "solution talk," or is willing to try out new behaviors or report on using new behaviors outside the group, the leader can reaffirm this effort and encourage discussion about the results.

As described by group therapy expert Yalom (2005), a leader's task is to use the following four sequences to lead to insight and understanding, as a foundation to support change:

- *Here is what your behavior looks like.* As addressed through feedback and self-observation, the patients learn to see themselves as others see them.

- *Here is how your behavior makes others feel.* The individual members learn about the impact of their actions on other members.

- *Here is how your behavior influences the opinions others have of you.* The members learn that because of their behavior, other people value them, dislike them, find them unpleasant, respect them, or avoid them.

- *Here is how your behavior influences your opinion of yourself.* Building on the information gathered in the first three steps, patients perform their own self-evaluations. They make judgments about their self-worth and their ability to be loved.

Fellowship (Mutual Help) Groups Versus Therapy Groups

There are many similarities as well as crucial differences between mutual help groups and therapy groups, and the two should not be confused. Among the many common elements between these groups are: sharing personal information, group discussion, self-identification, the challenging of misconceptions, imparting new information, socialization, and self-examination of one's behavior. Unlike therapy groups, fellowship groups such as Alcoholics Anonymous (AA) and Narcotics Anonymous (NA) provide important supports for recovery following principles, not absolute rules, and informally teach people new social and behavioral skills without drug use. Fellowship group leaders are selected from the membership; there are no professional standards, no expert professional advice, no supervision, no treatment plans, no record keeping, and no fees. In chemical dependency mutual help groups, the focus is on abstinence plus change of self to support recovery. Most mutual help groups use a leader-centered approach, where the "chair" calls upon people to share their personal stories or directs the discussion topic of that group meeting. The principles and steps for recovery are not theoretical; rather, they are practical concepts derived from current and past members' experiences and traditions. People discuss how they realized they had an addiction and how they can become abstinent, with an indirect effect of helping new members recognize their own limitations and illness. The group serves to offer hope and support for recovery. There is little or no emphasis on the exploration of emotions, feelings, and psychological problems underlying drug use problems.

Unlike a fellowship group, a therapy group is based on clinical practice and uses theoretically based models of behavior and change. The methods include interventions aimed at the behavior of the group as a whole, at individual members, and at subgroups. The group is subject to standards of professional practice with oversight from a clinical supervisor. While psychoeducation and task groups are often leader-centered, interactional groups allow members to select topics related to the group task (recovery) and lets issues unfold over time. Members will also learn to give specific behavioral feedback to one another and to tolerate conflict. Therapy groups define standards for acceptable group behavior, group goals, purpose, task, meeting times, and specific expectations. Group leaders develop treatment plans in collaboration with each member and maintain progress notes for each session. While there is attention to "how to recover," there is also emphasis on "what supports use and relapse." Therapy groups help members explore their emotions, psychological conflicts, behavior, and beliefs. There is usually a development of strong group cohesion among a core membership and progression through stages of group development, and an intense focus on each individual.

AA and Other 12-Step Groups

AA is a worldwide mutual aid society describing itself as a fellowship of men and women with a desire to stop drinking alcohol. They do this while helping others to do so through a program of "character development" by following the 12 Steps. (The teachings of the movement are described in *Alcoholics Anonymous Big Book, Fourth Edition* [2001].) The first of many 12-step programs, AA was started by white, middle-class Americans. It has a broad philosophy that aids AA in spreading "across diverse cultures holding different beliefs and values." AA has a tradition of remaining independent of other organizations and avoiding "outside issues." Although approximately two-fifths of people who participate in AA drop out within the first 3 months, its program is designed to help alcoholics maintain sobriety. What is important is that members pledge to "work the steps" and that they continue to attend meetings regularly for the best possible outcome.

AA celebrated its 75th anniversary in 2010. In 1934, AA cofounder Bill Wilson's drunkenness had ruined a promising career in finance, when a former drinking friend, Ebby Thacher, introduced Wilson to a spiritual solution for alcoholism that Thacher picked up as a member of the Oxford Group, a Christian society that promoted sobriety. Wilson subsequently stopped drinking for good. During a 1935 business trip to Akron, Ohio, Wilson's cravings for alcohol returned, and to stay sober, he met with another alcoholic, Dr. Bob Smith, and related how he stayed sober with the help of God. Wilson and Smith continued to meet and became convinced that working with other alcoholics helped them to stay sober. For the benefit of other alcoholics, they cofounded AA. The last day Smith drank alcohol, June 10, 1935, is the anniversary date of AA.

With all of the new scientific breakthroughs in understanding alcohol dependence (the scientific name for "alcoholism"), and with the recent development of medications to help patients, one might ask, *What is the future of AA?* As seen in Chapter 12, which deals with medications to aid recovery, current and evolving medications do not "cure" alcohol dependence. Rather, they reduce relapses, which are frequent in recovering alcohol-dependent patients. In other words, they do not prevent or instantly reverse the disease process. In all cases, usually after many years of drinking, new medications are taken to enhance current recovery methods. Thus, the damage to the patient's emotions, social relationships, health, and behavior has been building during the years of heavy alcohol consumption. Such damage will always require interventions such as AA.

AA also does not prevent or stop the disease process. What AA is so good at is "clearing away the wreckage of the past"—helping the sufferer overcome the effects of an immature, underdeveloped personality that essentially stopped developing at the age of the person's earliest drinking. Character development, making amends, learning how to evolve to a fully developed level of self-esteem, all without the use of alcohol, are the strengths of the AA recovery process. The strength and breadth of the current research on AA has reached such a high level that most scientists now believe that AA is an "evidence-based" program, meaning "proven effective by science".

For the foreseeable future, unless new medications are developed to totally prevent alcohol dependence, or to stop it in a brief period of time after it starts, AA will always be needed to help patients clear away the wreckage of the past. Indeed, today's medications do not work alone, and they will not cure the disease. They always require ongoing abstinence-based treatment (which often includes AA programs) or AA alone. (The Food and Drug Administration [FDA] requires that all current medications be used concurrently with ongoing abstinence-based treatment.)

Group Therapy and Co-occurring Disorders

Group therapy is effective for many patients with co-occurring disorders. The patient needs to be able to reasonably behave with others, to accept and provide feedback, to have a level of ego-strength (ability to tolerate having feelings or concerns dismissed or challenged by others), to tolerate anxiety, and to manage moderate conflict. Group composition is often better when all members have a co-occurring disorder versus a mixed group of co-occurring individuals and only drug use disorder individuals. Having co-leaders with expertise in drug use and mental health disorders care is vital.

Supportive confrontations (such as helping people identify discrepancies in their behavior) are appropriate; however, strong confrontation is contraindicated. An emphasis on emotional venting or catharsis will often result in members becoming fearful and abandoning the group. It is effective to use concrete, behavioral, and cognitive-oriented questions that allow patients to distance themselves from intense feelings and focus on less emotional issues. One approach might be to ask, *What would people like to talk about today?* Cognitive-oriented questions could include, *What do people think about what we discussed last time? What do people think about how the session ended last time? Is there any concern left over from last time that we need to revisit?*

A problem-solving group approach can be effective for patients with drug use disorders and major psychiatric disorders such as schizophrenia, major depression, and severe borderline personality disorder (BPD). This approach asks patients to identify concrete problems that interfere with their recovery from either drug use or their mental health disorder, and then to consider practical solutions. Depending upon the individual level of functioning, a problem-solving group may require a leader-centered process in which the leaders are actively directing the group discussion and focus. This can keep the members on task, focus on practical solutions, support group maintenance, and demonstrate appropriate behavior. Leaders should ask patients to identify or help one another identify concrete reasons to remain drug free (e.g., fewer hospitalizations, fewer mood swings, or fewer withdrawal symptoms).

The leaders may need to make frequent interventions with patients who become easily distracted by their symptoms, their anxiety, side effects of medications, or behaviors of other members of the group. If a person appears unfocused, confused, or disoriented, a concrete refocus to the present time and place can be helpful before moving to a new topic or task. For patients with a history of mania, it is important to monitor for evidence of grandiosity, agitation, rapid speech, restlessness, and magical beliefs in their own power, all of which suggest forthcoming mania. In dealing with patients with histories of confusion, delusion, or hallucinations, keeping tasks short and concrete and using visual aids are especially helpful.

A problem-solving group can provide education about 12-step principles, 12-step groups, and "double trouble" fellowship groups, and how these work. Patients with a history of magical thinking and religious delusions require care when discussing some 12-step concepts such as use of a "higher power." For patients with major depression who are suicidal or guilt ridden, caution is also required when discussing Step 4 (taking a fearless moral inventory), especially where there is a history of suicidal thoughts, severe guilt, or self-deprecation.

Patients who have chemical dependence with BPD can be successfully included in treatment groups if key principles are understood and applied. Because these individuals add great complexity to group dynamics, they can easily overwhelm even an experienced clinician, so a co-led treatment group is highly recommended.

When treating people with BPD in groups, clear rules for group interactions need to be reviewed frequently. Group leaders must work actively to prevent these patients from monopolizing the group discussion. When monopolizing occurs, the clinician should redirect the process by asking all group members to share their experiences; the clinician may have to interrupt or block the person with BPD from interrupting until all members have spoken. Group members should be encouraged to provide feedback about any obstructive or monopolizing behavior.

Group methods that are structured and teach social skills are helpful for patients with BPD. One common error is to constantly focus on their emotions and suspected "hidden" feelings. The patients struggle with intense emotions and have difficulty containing their feelings, which they then use to justify their extreme reactions. Group treatment must focus on helping these patients to contain and tolerate strong feelings. It is important, for example, to allow normal silences as therapeutic. Silence is frustrating to many patients, especially those with BPD, because it creates anxiety and evokes anger. However, this is also necessary to help them cope with feelings of emptiness and boredom, and it helps them think through their behavior. When these patients quickly break the silence, their action should be discussed in the group.

Due to the defense of "splitting," BPD patients may express strong anger toward a person in a session, yet an hour later respond as if their earlier emotions had not been expressed. This can cause havoc for group members and the group process if it is not discussed.

Group leaders need to assess their own reactions when dealing with BPD patients. Group leaders must be aware of and able to manage their feelings of anger and frustration because these patients will sense any hidden feelings and will internalize or externalize their reactions. Because BPD patients have trouble tolerating mixed emotional messages and ambivalence, they will become confused, frustrated, angry, or depressed. The treatment staff needs to be aware that whereas extreme behavior may be due to post-acute withdrawal or other symptoms of recovery, it is often an issue independent of chemical dependence recovery and requires additional attention.

Group Treatment With Mandated Patients

Group therapy with mandated patients can provide education and rehabilitation that supports an emphasis on change. While patients will learn about themselves and how to overcome their drug abuse, the primary goals of group treatment are assuming responsibility, being accountable, and making changes in behavior and thinking. Most mandated patients enter treatment with the view that it is "a task to complete" or "an obstacle to overcome" in pursuit of release on parole or release from probation supervision, and not a process of change.

Many mandated patients are anxious and fearful about change, yet may recognize the need to change, but will hide this fear using an aggressive or aloof appearance. One way to view resistance is in terms of being rebellious or rationalizing. Disdain for authority is common for rebellious patients, as demonstrated by procrastination and passive resistance to direction. These patients will identify with others who appear antisocial, from whom they gain emotional support and a sense of belonging. Rationalizing patients will always have an answer about why they cannot, do not, and should not change.

A group challenge may include asking people, *What do you need to do to convince the judge, parole officer, or probation officer that you no longer need to attend this program?* or *What will be required in order for you to convince them you no longer need to attend this program?*

The task of the group therapist is to help members recognize distortions in thinking and unacceptable behavior. Patients receive feedback from the group about self-defeating attitudes, beliefs, and behavior, and learn to try to use more effective ways to behave. Although patients are often resistant to change, attendance alone during group sessions tends to provoke change as patients learn to arrive at each session on time, work within group rules, and observe the effective behavior of others. Patients begin to make small gains that lead to completing long-term goals, rather than acting impulsively in an effort to gain immediate gratification.

An effective strategy with this population is to use groups to provide helpful and observable feedback, to focus on behavior and thinking, and to address thinking and behavior in the here and now. This focus helps patients identify and recognize behaviors, attitudes, and beliefs that precipitate drug use as well as criminal thinking and behavior. This approach also effectively lends itself to a focus on sobriety, which is best viewed as having a clear mind while thinking and behaving responsibly, not simply being abstinent.

Especially with patients who are mandated and likely rebellious, before asking questions or offering information, ask permission to do so. A common therapeutic error of group treatment with mandated patients is emphasizing abstinence and the need to make changes. Mandated patients are often developmentally akin to adolescents and any emphasis that appears like "someone pushing their agenda" is met with a rebellious response. The self-recognition of need for abstinence by some or most members will emerge on its own if the group is effectively managed. In addition, members will suppress any mention about their desire or thinking to use drugs.

It is an error to focus on "feelings and emotions," because many mandated patients operate more from a position of having status and feeling in command, impulsivity, readiness to use aggression, and action. It is more effective to shift to looking at perceptions, behavior, and thinking that leads to problems rather than behavior and thinking that keeps them out of trouble. For example, *Some of you said the judge ordered you into treatment and he was out to get you. What led you to decide that is true? What other reasons did the judges have for making that decision? If any were here now, what would they say were their reasons for ordering you into treatment? Would anyone else you know have agreed with that decision? What makes you say that?* If the patient is hostile and angry, a brief focus on those feelings and a more detailed focus on perceptions of being forced to attend treatment can be a useful counterresponse to negative responses.

The leader may wish to openly speculate about members' thoughts or feelings of being mandated and reflect these feelings and perceptions, then invite group members to explain the situation from their viewpoints.

CHAPTER 17

Involvement of the Family

with Peter J. Pociluyko, MA, CASAC, CCS

PATIENTS' OVERVIEW

Drug use disorders adversely affect not only the individual, they also impact those involved in the life of the person who is addicted. These social interactions influence and impact drug use, abstinence, relapse, and recovery.

It is widely recognized that family members will use various coping behaviors in response to a drug use disorder in a person. Understanding the effect of drug use disorders on family functioning and how family members may respond to disorder and periods of abstinence can help to promote important changes for the addicted person and family. In general, if one member of a social system changes (positively or negatively), the thinking, emotions, beliefs, and behavior of all others in that social system will change as well.

Family Structure

A family is best described as a social system of people linked together by a common history, who are interdependent, but need not be living together or in close proximity. Families across all cultures, societies, and faiths are organized in a consistent manner. A family will have a hierarchy, with those who hold greater levels of authority, knowledge, and responsibility than others, typically beginning with the senior adults at the top and youngest members at the bottom. There are also subsystems defined by generational boundaries, such as grandparents, parents, and children. The family will have boundaries (borders) such as knowledge, responsibilities, and abilities that adults or parents have or perform, but which children do not have or should not do. These boundaries cannot be too rigid, but must be permeable, so that children and adults can interact, and so that people are allowed to give or receive comfort, nurturing, and support. Just as individual behavior tends to be predictable and repeated, families behave according to fixed, nonrandom patterns of behavior that are largely automatic and unconscious. These nonrandom patterns are highly resistant to change and define unspoken and spoken rules about how "things work" within the family. Families have explicit and implicit unspoken beliefs about individual members, about how things are supposed to work, and about their identity as a system, which influences their individual and collective behavior. Family behavior, akin to biological processes, is homeostatic and self-correcting—the family will use consistent predictable behavior patterns (rules) to remain stable and prevent sudden change. Paradoxically, while a family must remain stable and predictable, the system cannot remain the same as people age, die, or leave; it must adapt and change as children grow up, gain new responsibilities, attend school, move away from home, as well as when new members join the family.

Family Disruption

A normal and functional family is disrupted when a member becomes disabled, dies, moves away, or cannot function. Typically, other members will assume that person's responsibilities and tasks. This action helps maintain stability and order in the system. All families develop automatic protective behaviors and responses that help to maintain a family's reputation and public image, and to protect individual or collective members from "outsiders." Such protective responses can also become automated to the point of reaction without rational thought and without conscious consideration of consequences.

When one or more members of a family develop a mental illness or drug use disorder, this can cause anxiety and confusion in the family structure. Anxiety and confusion are met by attempts to "overcontrol" the problem and by overfunctioning, or by "undercontrol" and underfunctioning, either of which may lead to psychological disorder, physical illness, and the use of drugs in others.

A common initial response of family members to a mental health or drug use disorder is to ignore the early symptoms or to explain the problem as due to an external cause such as "bad friends," school peers, a problem boss, or a stressful job. This rationalization can be followed by protective behaviors such as certain adults and children assuming added duties. Over time, this can become a permanent way of operating and prevents individual members from assuming appropriate or normal responsibilities.

In more severe cases, the family's hierarchy becomes confused or even inverted. For example, a child may feel the need to assume parenting functions and discipline of younger siblings. One or both parents may turn to children as confidants, sharing knowledge that should only be discussed with adults. As a result, children may be in a sensitive position of maintaining secrets from one parent, denying they have knowledge of it, and feeling loyal to one parent and disloyal to both parents at the same time. It is quite common in families for grandparents, uncles, or aunts to align with children and an adult partner against the person with a drug use disorder. This is called a "coalition"—a secret alliance across generational boundaries against a third party, and is a violation of a functional family hierarchy. If an adult or teenager has a drug use disorder, a parent or grandparent may cover for their drug use and their negative behaviors in order to protect them from consequences.

Parents, spouses, and children of drug abusers have commonly been observed to overfunction—as spouse, caregiver, and breadwinner. Children may respond to a parent's drug use disorder by avoidance and only interact with the nonaddicted parent. Some may do the opposite and assume a protective role of the person with the disorder and maintain distance from the more functional parent. Either of these scenarios places increased demands on the functional adults (and children) and frequently leads to feelings of depression and anxiety, followed by using or increasing tobacco, alcohol, antidepressants, and antianxiety medications.

Enabling behavior is commonly described as pathological or dysfunctional; however, this behavior in a social system such as a family is actually functional and done for an important purpose. Enabling is specifically done out of concern and fear that something terrible will happen if this "help" is not given to the person with a drug use disorder. Enabling is also a gesture of affection—"to protect Sallie from getting worse." This feeling of affection and concern alternates with feelings of anger, frustration, distrust, and disappointment. Enabling is, more important, a way to maintain predictable behavior and emotional stability within the family.

Engaging Family Members

At some point in the treatment of the person with a drug use disorder, the family will be informed of an opportunity to learn about the treatment process and will be allowed to ask questions and even to be involved in family therapy. At this time, if family members agree to be involved, a clinician will help family members understand the nature of treatment and how the drug user will change because of the treatment.

A clinician must recognize and overcome any negative biases and assumptions about families and addicted patients and maintain a balanced, objective, and detached view. A useful view is to see the dysfunctional family as protective, with well-meaning intentions and actions that inadvertently support the person's drug use. On the other hand, some family members do recognize the drug use problem and are not so willing to protect the drug user from natural consequences.

A major challenge is to convince the patient to allow the clinician to contact and meet with family members. Sometimes patients will claim they are not involved with their family or that they see them infrequently. Usually this is not true and is an attempt to protect the family from blame or to avoid exposure of family problems; people addicted to drugs have strong connections and regular interactions with parents, siblings, grandparents, or related family members. A useful engagement strategy is to say, *Your family members are really important and know many ways to help you. So with your permission, I would like to talk to them.* This may have to be stated many times before the patient consents and allows the clinician access to the family. If the patient claims the family is not interested in a session or won't come, the clinician should offer to invite family members personally. A useful strategy is to tell family members, *You know the person better than anyone else. I would like to seek your wisdom and expertise to help him recover.* The clinician can also tell the family that previous attempts to help the addict without involving the family simply have not worked. Sometimes family members report they were never asked their opinion, never asked to come for sessions, or if they attended they may have felt blamed.

As the addicted person begins recovery, there will be a desire to resume some or all of the roles as parent, spouse, student, oldest child, and so on. This will be met with overt and covert resistance. Children of adults with a drug use disorder may enjoy having significant responsibility and power even if they have assumed responsibilities far beyond what their age or experience allows. Having these adult responsibilities enhances a child's status and self-esteem, becomes a part of their identity; many children will not readily relinquish these roles and responsibilities. Some may think they are "adults." Some family members may have been overinvolved (enmeshed) with one another, almost to the point of "emotional smothering"; others may be detached and disengaged; and still others will fluctuate between ambivalent states of being enmeshed and being disengaged.

Family members and the drug user can become fixed in certain behaviors and assume rigid roles that were once functional, but which also do not support recovery and may even be unhelpful to other family members. The family's hierarchy can become confused or even inverted (upside down). One task of the clinician can be to understand how the family currently operates, then help people define and begin to use new roles and structures that can help the family operate better.

Basic Family Interviewing Strategies

Here are some general tips for the clinician.

- Be certain to compliment people for coming to the session and taking time from a busy schedule to attend.
- Say something about the family's assets, insights, perceptions, apparent intelligence, and so on that might include their willingness to "go to the mat" to help the chemically dependent person.
- Help people identify and talk about solutions, not just problems.
- Avoid labeling people as dysfunctional, as "enablers"; or labeling children as the "family hero," "lost child," and so on. Look for their strengths and assets, not their pathology.
- Do not assume you know what people mean by their use of terminology or figures of speech. Ask people to clarify and explain their use of terminology and avoid presuming that you know what the patient or family member means by their street expressions: *You mentioned he does not listen to you. So that I can understand, what would I see if that occurs and how would I know he is not listening to you?*
- Language tense, verb use, and tone are important because these can communicate important messages of a hope, an outcome, or expectations. Instead of using dismissive words such as "but," "however," and "although," use words with inclusive or positive connotation such as "and," "in addition," "simultaneously," or "it also seems." For example: *"So he is smart and he developed problems by getting mixed up with drugs."*

Addiction Essentials

• Use *"So far"* at the beginning of the sentence to imply change is possible: *So far, things are working OK, improving, progressing.* Use *"yet"* at the end of the sentence to hint that change has not occurred but will at some later point: *So you have not been able to remain abstinent just yet.* Use past tense comments to talk about problems or negative behaviors, or to refer to old solutions that did not work: *So last year (last month, yesterday, and so on) he was not doing well and the methods you described did not work.* Use present and future tense to talk about change and when things are better. Also use language to indicate that two opposite positions may both be true at the same time: *So while his drinking and drug use upsets you, at the same time you can predict how he will act and plan your next step.*

• Ask people about their perceptions and to be accountable for the details: *You said his grandmother covers up for him. Are you certain that is her goal?* Use reframing to attribute positive intention to a behavior that is seen only in a negative manner. Reframing can also be used to therapeutically imply a negative perspective about unhelpful behavior. For example, reframe enabling as protective behavior or as "loving too much and preventing learning from consequences." Or reframe as irresponsible a family member's refusal to seek treatment that disrupts other members' lives.

• Use exception questions to identify when the drug use problem is less severe or not imposing problems, and to identify what people are doing that may be helpful: *When is this drug problem less severe? What is different on days when the drinking or drug use is not a problem or is less of a problem? What did you do differently? What difference did your actions have on your own or others' drug use? So what is different since our last session? What is better? What is the same? Is anything worse? What specifically is better? What difference did that method have?*

• Use presupposition questions to imply that change can occur and to help people define what would be a positive outcome: *When this problem is under control and things are going well for your family (your relationship, and so on), what will tell you things are better?*

Basic Family Counseling Principles and Strategies

Whereas family therapy requires specialized training and formal licensure, many addiction clinicians can provide rudimentary family counseling services, couples counseling, and family education. Even though family counseling is not a 12-step support for family members, as are

Al-Anon and Nar-Anon, many times family members can benefit from attending these types of meetings, along with family counseling and education.

There is a process of "joining" a family system, and once a family feels the clinician has made a connection, it is easier to engage the family and make interventions. When first contacting or interviewing members, begin by recognizing and respecting the leaders of the family by addressing them first. If a grandmother or mother is the most senior adult, she should be presumed to be the strongest in the family's power structure. Then it is appropriate to address the next older adult, then any other adult and older adolescents, and ask the parent to introduce the younger children. Also pay attention to who speaks for the family or who speaks for certain individuals, because this may define a specific rule of how the family operates. Ask permission to engage in a conversation with a specific member: *"Is it OK if I ask your youngest son a few questions?"* Genuinely complimenting people is equally vital.

Helping the family reestablish hierarchy and proper boundaries is a key task. For example, in a family with a parent in recovery, if it appears children are treated as confidants by one or both parents or when parents are present in the room, or an oldest child is allowed or asked to control or discipline the younger siblings, this should be noted for future intervention. It is necessary to refer to the specific behavior as protective, helpful, or supportive—behavior that was probably started due to a parent's drug use disorder. One intervention involves commenting on age-appropriate roles for children and noting that an older child is still doing the job of a parent who is now in recovery. This is followed by advising parents that it is time they reassume their adult roles and responsibilities to "unburden their children." Another intervention is suggesting that parents only discuss adult and marital issues with each other and with the clinician or family therapists, and not with the children.

When adolescents and young adults are in treatment, one method is to explain to the overinvolved parent or grandparent that despite his or her hard work, "doing it all alone" has not worked and a new approach is needed. The enmeshed parent or grandparent may be asked "to agree to take a vacation" and temporarily "defer monitoring" to another adult or parent. If agreed, then the disengaged adult is asked to take charge for the next several weeks. This must be done diplomatically so the enmeshed adult or grandparent "saves face" and is not blamed for supporting or compounding the person's drug use. This intervention can help reduce the overinvolved relationship between the enmeshed parent or grandparent and the drug user, to set up a boundary between the adults and the patient, and to help realign the family hierarchy by drawing the adult figures into a mutual alliance to help the patient.

One strategy is requiring the "distant adult" to take the lead in monitoring the patient's treatment, ensuring session attendance, ensuring urinalysis tests, and perhaps taking the person to fellowship meetings. This will indirectly educate family members about AA or NA, engage the patient and the detached parent, and set the stage for change if any adults also have a drug use disorder. It could also include asking the monitoring adult to log how the patient appears or sounds each day (i.e., does the person seem to be using or not?). It could also include monitoring a patient's treatment activity to ensure timely arrival and staying for the entire session. The family can be given some type of weekly task that may include daily conversations for 10 min with the patient about activities, actions, and recovery efforts.

Changes in a family system will lead to some distress due to realignment, until people stabilize into new roles and patterns. A family crisis will nearly always occur within weeks after an adolescent, adult, or spouse begins recovery and the family roles and structure begin to shift. In general, if some form of a family crisis does not occur shortly after recovery begins, then the family structure change is probably not occurring. Family crises, just like relapses, are not failures in treatment, but are key signs that the treatment is evoking change. A crisis could be a major fight between spouses or parents, threats of separation or divorce, a conflict between one adult and a parent, a family member who becomes suicidal, or the emergence of a family member with a psychiatric or addiction problem that was not obvious. It is helpful to tell the family to expect periodic crises during recovery or while a plan of recovery is being implemented, but that these crises should not stop the support of a patient's recovery. Family crises can be used as excuses to explain why an assigned task (e.g., taking the patient to a treatment session) could not be carried out. It is then that the adults should be firmly urged to cooperate for the sake of the patient. In general, if some form of family crisis does not occur shortly after recovery begins, then a change in the family structure is probably not occurring and perhaps the patient has returned to using.

Basic Counseling Strategies With Couples

Whether working with married spouses, heterosexual couples living together unmarried, committed gay or lesbian couples, or common-law spouses, working with couples is important and the methods are essentially the same for all of these situations. Conjoint counseling is best provided after the patient with a drug use problem is in a state of remission for at least a few weeks or a month. It does not require months of abstinence before these conjoint sessions are provided, and in fact it is best to initiate these earlier rather than later.

Most couples behave differently when one member stops using drugs than when the person is abstinent. Many times each partner will be able to identify the adaptive or drug-induced behaviors in the other person, but cannot recognize their own adaptive responses to the person's drug use. With careful observation and questioning, many couples can learn to recognize and interrupt old nonfunctional behavioral patterns. Helping both parties learn new productive behaviors without being under the influence of a psychoactive drug will improve their relationship. This helps reduce the risk of relapse.

As with families, both members of a couple contribute to and maintain functional and maladaptive behavior (A influences B, and B influences A). One person does not cause the other's drug use disorder, yet they both help maintain the supporting patterns of behavior. A couple under stress or conflict becomes unstable, unless both parties know how to resolve differences. Many couples experiencing relationship-based stress will create a triad to help stabilize the relationship. One example of a triad is when one spouse routinely discusses concerns with a friend, a coworker, a parent, a child, or a therapist but not with the partner. In fact, each member of a couple may have one or more confidants to whom they vent their frustration. Triads stabilize a troubled dyadic relationship, but unfortunately prevent the couples from directly facing and resolving conflict.

During a couples therapy session, one strategy is to have the members face each other, and have a direct discussion about one significant problem they both agree needs to be resolved. This task usually brings out normal "at home behavior" and allows the clinician to see escalating and counterproductive behavior firsthand. Once these behaviors are identified, the clinician can help the couple change dysfunctional patterns that govern their relationship. New behavior must be learned while in a drug-free state. Additionally, asking a couple to hold hands while discussing their concerns can be an effective way to increase intimacy and emotional intensity.

Due to drug use disorders, people in a relationship stop comforting and supporting each other. One method to overcome this is using "caring days," a technique to help the couple identify and request supportive and comforting behaviors. The therapist asks each partner to list as many behaviors as possible that would be a sign of love or affection: *I like to be taken to lunch on a workday once in a while. I like to get unexpected cards or flowers once in a while. I like to be called at work, even for a minute or two, to see how my day is going.* Once the lists are compiled, the parties exchange them. The couple is told that they may not ask for or expect any behavior on the list. They are also told that each is free to perform as many or as few of the behaviors as desired. Because each partner will want to be viewed as a caring partner, many of the desired behaviors will be carried out before the next session. This will produce positive changes in the relationship.

Many other strategies have been developed and can be used by skilled family therapists and addiction clinicians with more advanced family therapy training.

CHAPTER 18

Relapse and Relapse Prevention

PATIENTS' OVERVIEW

It is important for the patient to understand that relapse is a part of the disease of chemical dependence. What formerly used to be called "getting worse" or "deterioration of the person" is now a sign of the disease, expected but not always seen, for reasons based mainly on the neurochemistry of the patient"s brain. While clinicians and scientists continue to search for the exact cause of relapses, they recognize that drug cues and environmental cues play a large role in relapse. Most importantly, relapse prevention is now an established part of treatment aftercare. Any treatment center that does not include a meaningful relapse prevention plan as part of the patient's treatment is setting the patient up for a less-than-complete chance of full recovery.

Relapse technically means "the reappearance of symptoms of a disease after a disease-free period." In the case of chemical dependence ("addiction"), a person who relapses begins using the drug again after a period of abstinence. Older definitions have been used for addiction: "get worse," "deteriorate," "going back to bad behavior," "becoming a criminal again"—these are now incorrect.

Chemical dependence ("addiction") is a chronic, relapsing illness. Its relapse rates are similar to those of other chronic diseases such as asthma, diabetes, and hypertension. Relapses occur either during or after treatment, requiring treatment adjustment or reinstatement. Relapses are sometimes seen as failures of treatment, but scientifically we know that relapses are a part of the recovery process in many people. Especially for friends and family members of the recovering person, it is important to recognize that the relapsing person is not "losing his willpower" or "slipping"; rather, it is to be expected in vulnerable patients, just as new tumors might pop up in a recovering cancer patient. The analogy with cancer here is perfect: Neither person in recovery expects a relapse, nor do they desire it, nor do they have much control over it.

Causes of Relapse

There are two general causes of relapse: physiological and psychosocial. Both causes probably contribute to relapse in most people.

Because chemical dependence is a chronic brain disease, the cause of the disease is at the level of the nerve cells (neurons) in the part of the brain called the "reward pathway." Neuroscience research says that the cause of the disease is dysregulation of the neurons in the pathway, related to short- or long-term neuroadaptations through chronic drug exposure plus (in many cases) genetic vulnerability. Thus there is a structural change in some component of the reward pathway that causes people to lose control over the use of a drug. We can understand, then, that this process did not take place overnight or even over weeks or months. Thus it is clear that the process cannot be reversed in a short period of time, such as months, and sometimes not years. As treatment progresses, there is a hill-and-valley effect during which a person will feel "more sober" (less troubled) on some days and "less sober" (more troubled) on others. During the periods of "less sober," the person's defenses are down and there is more vulnerability to relapse.

In chemical terms, a patient's cellular functioning could also cycle, with the "hill" reflecting a "more normal" functioning, and a "valley" reflecting a "less normal" functioning of the reward system. Cycles of cell function and metabolism occur in all body systems, often associated with neurochemical or hormonal fluctuations in these systems. Such fluctuations are under the influence of the individual's environment: food intake, stress, amount of rest, and others.

Animal studies have shown that the environment plays a strong role in brain-chemistry functioning. For example, rats trained to sit in a cage for 15 minutes before receiving access to a drug (e.g., alcohol) show increased levels of dopamine in microdialysis tubes as they sit and wait for the drug reward. (Microdialysis is a micromethod of painlessly measuring dopamine in effluents coming from the tip of a probe placed into the brain's reward pathway.) It is well known that increased levels of dopamine are related to the effects of alcohol and other drugs, perhaps related to the "pleasure" produced by the drugs. For an animal trained to wait for a drug reward, we can conclude that an increased amount of dopamine during the waiting period reflects an "anticipation" to getting the drug. This is similar to (for example) a cocaine-dependent person "anticipating" the next hit of cocaine, even if the person is in recovery. In general, the greater the quality of recovery or the higher the resistance of the person to relapse, the less the person will "anticipate" another drug episode. Contributing to the "resistance" to relapse is the natural cycling of the dopamine function in the brain throughout the day.

The word *cues* is used a great deal when describing or trying to prevent relapse. Cues for a drug user or chemically dependent person involve triggers in the environment that are highly salient (meaningful) because of a person's drug use history. Thus, for a person in recovery from alcohol dependence, a bar, a former drinking partner, or an advertisement for beer, wine, or a particular brand of spirit might be a powerful trigger (cue). People in solid, long-term recovery from alcohol dependence are usually not significantly affected by old cues. In fact, they often use the exposure to old cues as a challenge to indicate that they are much better than they used to be.

Triggers are particularly powerful to people in recovery from cigarettes, cocaine, and heroin. Thus for a smoker to be in a situation where they formerly smoked (after a meal, with an alcoholic drink, after sex) is a challenge to keep from smoking. This is confounded by the "habit" (reduced willpower) associated with smoking: The act of lighting up, the act of taking a drag on the cigarette, the taste of the burning tobacco, the exhalation of smoke, and other powerful cues add to the difficulty of giving up cigarettes for good. *The habit is not even the killer—it is the carcinogens in the smoke! If I could just use a cigarette without the nicotine and smoke, I wouldn't have to quit!*

For cocaine and heroin, the cues are much more related to friends, places, and drug paraphernalia. The "crack corner," the "pipe," the glass tubes: These are the real triggers to relapse for a "hard drug" user. The statement we hear most often is, *Just getting the "stuff" ready to use is a bigger turn-on than actually taking the drug!* Could it be that "getting the stuff ready" is similar to a rat being placed in a cage for 15 min before getting the drug? And that both situations cause an increase in dopamine in the brain's reward pathway before the drug is taken? And that this increase in dopamine in the reward pathway reduces the resistance of the recovering person to use the drug, leading to relapse? These and other questions make sense in light of current neurobiological research, but much more research is necessary to finalize this speculative conclusion.

A Family System View of Relapse

Many professionals view a drug use lapse (brief return to use) and a relapse as part of a neurobiological disease process. While an intense desire and action to return to use is often directly due to drug-induced changes in the brain and psychological effects, marital or family dynamics also have a significant influence on emotions and thinking that will support lapses and relapse. Because the disease of chemical dependence is a complex biopsychosocial disorder, relapse often needs to be viewed as more than a biological or psychological response to drug-induced brain changes.

Many times despite negative effects on the individual, a person's problem may also provide some automatic protective and functional effect for the family, marriage, or committed couple's relationship. The individual problem can also be a metaphor for other family problems. For example, a drug use disorder of one member often effectively helps to hide and call attention away from serious problems of other family members. The patient's problem may also distract other family members from their own serious difficulties. Family therapy research with adults and adolescents shows that one or more members of the family may have some significant problem (drug use disorder, depression, anxiety disorder) or conflict (i.e., family conflict, domestic violence). These "other problems" are kept at bay when the family's attention is focused on the person with a drug problem. Once a patient begins recovery, family conflicts or other serious problems can come to the surface. A family or couple's relationship may then begin to destabilize, or a family member may start to decompensate (deteriorate). If the patient lapses or relapses, the family will tend to refocus on the patient and will collectively and individually restabilize as they set aside other difficulties. This pattern of attempted recovery, family disruption, relapse, and restabilizing often appears as a repeating pattern that may occur many times over months or years. The patient's problem can also be a reflection of problems of other family members who have a drug use or mental disorder.

It is often difficult to observe these family patterns because they may occur as an escalating pattern over days or weeks. However, they can be reconstructed from family interviews about what was happening with each family member over the preceding period.

In the following example, an adult woman has lived with her parents, is abstinent, stable, and resides in a halfway house. She has been abstinent for 5 months and has never had more than a month's abstinence prior to this point. During regular phone conversations with her parents, it becomes evident that the parents are expressing increased levels of marital discord, perhaps threats of separation or divorce. This has been going on for years, but no action was taken and the conflict was "set aside" due to their daughter's progressive drug use disorder. In response to the parents' troubles, the woman feels stressed, begins to violate house rules, soon returns to drug use, and then attempts suicide by overdose. Immediately, the parents drop their conflict to again focus on the daughter.

Relapse Prevention

The goals of relapse prevention must be (a) quality initial treatment, (b) participation in support programs during and after treatment, (c) reduction in cue-related triggers for relapse, and (d) the identification of warning signs that begin long before recurring drug use. The ideal situation would be for the chemically dependent patient to enroll in a high-quality medically based inpatient treatment or intensive outpatient center for longer than 30 days, then after initial treatment to move to a new neighborhood with supportive family or friends, and be monitored by a recovery management team. This would have all the necessary characteristics: quality long-term treatment involving support programs during and after care, reduced drug use cues, and a recovery management team that can identify the early signs of relapse.

Relapse prevention is critical, because many who relapse subsequently die in a drug overdose situation or in a long-term drug use situation that declines to death. There also may be physical or emotional collapse or suicide. The well-respected CENAPS (acronym for Center for Applied Behavioral Sciences) model of relapse prevention therapy teaches patients to "recognize and manage warning signs of relapse and to interrupt the relapse progression early and return to positive progress in recovery." The primary goals of CENAPS are to (a) assess the global lifestyle patterns contributing to relapse, (b) construct a personalized list of relapse warning signs, (c) develop warning sign management strategies, (d) develop a structured recovery program to identify and manage warning signs, and (e) develop a relapse early intervention plan.

It is now well known that extended abstinence is predictive of sustained recovery in which relapse is greatly reduced. According to one study, about two-thirds of people relapse at least once during the first year of abstinence, and it takes a year before less than half (one-third) relapse. After 5 years of abstinence, the chance for relapse declines to less than 15%. In fact, brain scans have shown that with recovery from methamphetamine dependence, the function in critical brain areas is almost completely restored—although continuing recovery management is necessary to overcome the negative psychological effects of long-term usage of this dangerous chemical.

What Is Recovery?

We now know that "full" recovery is a challenge for most people, especially those who began their drug use early or who were in the throes of the disease for a long time before they sought treatment. Thus, most people after treatment are in various stages of recovery as they go through life.

There is almost no research on recovery because previously there was never a definition of *recovery*. In 2006, the Betty Ford Institute convened a consensus conference of important researchers and people in recovery to develop a definition of *recovery*. The purpose was to promote research on this critical topic, so that scientists would be able to measure and improve upon the means to recovery. The definition is as follows: "Recovery from substance dependence is a voluntarily maintained lifestyle characterized by sobriety, personal health, and citizenship (Betty Ford Institute Consensus Panel, 2007, p. 222)." *Sobriety* is defined as abstinence from alcohol, nicotine, and all other nonprescribed drugs. Duration is important: *early sobriety* (1–12 months), *sustained sobriety* (1–5 years), and *stable sobriety* (5 years or more). "Personal health" refers to an improved quality of personal life—physical health, psychological health, independence, and spirituality as measured by quality-of-life scales. *Citizenship* refers to living with regard and respect for those around you—social function and environment as measured by quality-of-life scales. Today, the best method to achieve recovery is through abstinence, although this may change as researchers delve further into the meaning and definition of *recovery*. It is clear that abstinence from drugs is not recovery, but abstinence is the beginning of recovery. Nor is sobriety the same as recovery. Sobriety seems to be the beginning of full recovery, but other qualities are also necessary. For example, many people who are "sober" are still struggling with "serenity"—the holy grail of recovery. It is likely that many people who are happy, sober, and drug-free will continue to struggle with this quality for the rest of their lives—just as many people without the disease do today. This is because serenity is a goal for almost everyone.

There are former drug users who rarely think about their favorite drug anymore. These include some "alcoholics," smokers, cocaine and crack "addicts," and heroin "addicts" in recovery. On the other hand, there are former drug users in the late stages of life who are still struggling to find sobriety and serenity. The wide range of trials, tribulations, emotions, and life outcomes is probably best explained by the fact that many in recovery are former drug "abusers" who did not have a brain disease but who chose to use drugs and then stop—many needing good 12-step programs or high-priced treatment to achieve abstinence. Others in recovery are those who have a brain disease—chemically dependent patients whose brains are more resistant to full recovery and must work hard at it almost every day. Finally there are others in recovery who are dependent on maintenance medications to control their cravings for drugs and to maintain a good quality of life. These individuals may have a severe form of dependence that requires a daily chemical to overcome the permanent dysregulation of brain function that is a part of their lives. In theory, those users and abusers who have mild or moderate disorder are easier to treat than chemically dependent individuals who have a moderate or severe form of the disease.

The good news is that you can find people in quality recovery wherever you go, and the hope of sobriety and recovery is what others continue to seek—often successfully. It is important for everyone to understand that chemical dependence ("addiction") is a brain disease—and that it can be successfully treated.

Resources for Readers

PATIENTS' OVERVIEW

The background, predicaments, and needs of patients with substance use disorders vary as widely as their personalities. Because this book cannot provide all the answers that patients have, we provide herein extra resources that may add to the knowledge. Patients, however, should be careful about using information from nonreviewed or laymen's sources. In addition, clinicians may have therapeutic experiences that differ from what would be expected based upon public literature. Members of the patient's team should be aware of all medications, nutraceuticals, and over-the-counter products that the patient may be using.

Those who read this book do so for various reasons: personal, educational, or professional, or perhaps out of curiosity. For those who want more, the following resources will help. The resources are current at this time, but material in this field goes out-of-date quickly. I suggest that if you find a Web site address that is outdated, you should go back to the original source (for example, find the site using a search engine) to find and update your knowledge.

Some Favorite Web sites

1. *Federal agencies* that fund research on alcohol and other drugs, and from which you can receive a lot of free information. In addition, some

of the information on these Web sites is in the public domain, which means that you don't need copyright permission to make copies or distribute it (unless you're charging for the information). Copyrighted material is indicated where appropriate on the Web site.

National Institute on Alcohol Abuse and Alcoholism:
    http://www.niaaa.nih.gov/
National Institute on Drug Abuse:
    http://www.nida.nih.gov/ *or*
    http://www.drugabuse.gov/
Substance Abuse and Mental Health Services Administration
    (SAMHSA): http://www.samhsa.gov/
U.S. Food and Drug Administration: http://www.fda.gov/
U.S. Food and Drug Administration Tobacco Products site:
    http://www.fda.gov/TobaccoProducts/default.htm

2. *Academic Web sites* that provide educational materials about alcohol and other drug abuse and dependence.

Addiction Research Center, University of Michigan Department
    of Psychiatry: http://www.psych.med.umich.edu/
Addiction Science Research and Education Center, The University of Texas at Austin: http://www.utexas.edu/asrec/research/
Bowles Center for Alcohol Studies, The University of North
    Carolina at Chapel Hill School of Medicine:
    http://www.med.unc.edu/alcohol/
Center for Alcohol & Addiction Studies, Brown University:
    http://www.caas.brown.edu/
Research Institute on Addictions, University of Buffalo:
    http://www.ria.buffalo.edu/
Pearson Center for Alcoholism & Addiction Research, The
    Scripps Research Institute, La Jolla:
    http://www.pearsoncenter.org/index.html
Treatment Research Institute, The University of Pennsylvania
    Center for the Studies of Addiction:
    http://www.tresearch.org/
UCLA Integrated Substance Abuse Programs, Los Angeles:
    http://www.uclaisap.org/
Waggoner Center for Alcohol & Addiction Research,
    The University of Texas at Austin:
    http://www.utexas.edu/research/wcaar/

3. *Research organization Web sites* that illustrate the active research being carried out on alcohol and other drug problems. These are mostly for members, although the Web sites have a public area and a place to donate money to support the work of the organization.

American College of Neuropsychopharmacology:
  http://www.acnp.org/
Association for Medical Education and Research in Substance
  Abuse (AMERSA): http://www.amersa.org/
Research Society on Alcoholism: http://www.rsoa.org/
Texas Research Society on Alcoholism:
  http://www.rsoa.org/trsa.htm
College on Problems of Drug Dependence:
  http://www.cpdd.vcu.edu/

4. *How to find a treatment center.* The federal SAMHSA site is an unbiased site to facilitate finding a treatment center in your area.

SAMHSA Substance Abuse Treatment Facility Locator:
  http://dasis3.samhsa.gov/

5. *Trade organization,* with listings of the top treatment centers in the nation.

National Association for Addiction Treatment Providers:
  http://www.naatp.org/

6. *Treatment centers,* illustrating the range of nonprofit centers available. Representative treatment centers are listed, and are not necessarily endorsed by the author of this book.

Betty Ford Center, Rancho Mirage, CA:
  http://www.bettyfordcenter.org/index.php
Caron, several locations: http://www.caron.org/
Edgewood, Nanaimo, British Columbia, Canada:
  http://www.edgewood.ca/
Hazelden, Center City, MN: http://www.hazelden.org/
Sundown M Ranch, Yakima, WA: http://www.sundown.org/

7. *Miscellaneous, not-for-profit organizations* with Web sites that are full of interesting information.

ATTC Network, committed to helping the public and those in the field stay abreast of what works in treatment and prevention: www.nattc.org

Betty Ford Institute, an outgrowth of the Betty Ford Treatment Center. This institute supports research and education on prevention, treatment, and recovery topics. A Web site feature is SciMat (Science and Research Matters in the Battle Against Addictive Disease), which highlights research articles written in understandable language: http://www.bettyfordinstitute.org/

Faces and Voices of Recovery, an advocacy organization for people in recovery: http://www.facesandvoicesofrecovery.org/

Join Together, the top U.S. Web site for keeping up-to-date with scientific and policy advances on a daily basis, written for professionals and the general public. After typing your e-mail address in the "Stay Informed" box on the home page, you will receive daily updates on hot topics in the field: http://www.jointogether.org/

Motivational Interviewing Web site—the main Web site with free resources on motivational interviewing (MI), with access to many resources including books, training, and inexpensive VHS or DVD demonstrations of MI techniques: www.motivationalinterviewing.org

National Council on Alcoholism and Drug Dependence, a voluntary health organization dedicated to fighting alcoholism and addiction: http://ncadd.org/

Many sites now offer social media access as well. For example, you could check to see if your favorite sites have Twitter or Facebook access.

8. *Scientific journals* of interest to practitioners and graduate students (peer-reviewed).

Addiction: http://www.addictionjournal.org/
Addiction Biology:
    http://www.wiley.com/bw/journal.asp?ref=1355-6215
Addictive Behaviors: http://www.elsevier.com/wps/find/
    journaldescription.cws_home/471/description#description
Alcohol: http://journals.elsevierhealth.com/periodicals/alc/home
Alcohol and Alcoholism: http://alcalc.oxfordjournals.org/
Alcoholism: Clinical and Experimental Research:
    http://www.wiley.com/bw/journal.asp?ref=0145-6008

Alcoholism Treatment Quarterly: http://www.informaworld.com/
smpp/title~content=t792303970~db=all

American Journal of Drug and Alcohol Abuse: http://www
.informaworld.com/smpp/title~content=t713597226~db=all

American Journal on Addictions: http://www.informaworld.com/
smpp/title~content=t713665609~db=all

Drug and Alcohol Dependence: http://www.elsevier.com/wps/find/
journaldescription.cws_home/506052/description#description

Drug and Alcohol Review: http://www3.interscience.wiley.com/
journal/122413760/grouphome/home.html

Journal of Addictions Nursing: http://www.informaworld.com/
smpp/title~content=t713669403

Journal of Addictive Diseases: http://www.informaworld.com/
smpp/title~content=t792306884~db=all

Journal of Drug Education: http://www.baywood.com/journals/
previewjournals.asp?id=0047-2379

Journal of Psychoactive Drugs: http://www.journalofpsychoactive-
drugs.com/

Journal of Social Work Practice in the Addictions: http://www.
informaworld.com/smpp/title~content=t792306973~db=all

Journal of Substance Abuse: http://www.sciencedirect.com/sci-
ence/journal/08993289

Journal of Substance Abuse Treatment:
http://www.elsevier.com/wps/find/journaldescription
.cws_home/525475/description#description

Journal of Substance Use: http://www.informaworld.com/smpp/
title~content=t713655978

Journal of Studies on Alcohol and Drugs: http://www.jsad.com/

Journal of Teaching in the Addictions: http://www.informaworld
.com/smpp/title~content=t792306974~db=all

Nicotine & Tobacco Research: http://ntr.oxfordjournals.org/

Psychology of Addictive Behaviors:
http://www.apa.org/pubs/journals/adb/

Substance Abuse: http://www.informaworld.com/smpp/
title~content=t792306970~db=all

Substance Use & Misuse: http://www.informaworld.com/smpp/
title~content=t713597302~db=all

For many of the journals listed above, you can be added to the Table of Contents alert list for each issue by going to the journal's site and registering.

While Wikipedia is an interesting source of information, one should use caution in referring to this Web site as accurate, especially scientifically. It is not a peer-reviewed Web site and often incorrect information can be found there. This site is a good one to begin searching for something new, but all information should be confirmed before using it for any purpose.

To find new scientific articles on addiction in any of the above journals, and others not listed:

National Institutes of Health, National Library of Medicine: www.pubmed.gov

Some Books for Practitioners, Graduate Students, and Patients

The following group is related to pharmacology, addiction disease process, and diagnostics.

1. American Psychiatric Association (2000). *Diagnostic and Statistical Manual of Mental Disorders* (4th ed., text revision) (DSM-IV-TR). Washington, DC: Author.
2. Brick, J., & Erickson, C. K. (1999). *Drugs, the brain, and behavior:* The pharmacology of abuse and dependence. Binghamton, NY: Haworth Press.
3. Brick, J. (Ed.) (2008). *Handbook of the medical consequences of alcohol and drug* (2nd ed.). New York, NY: Haworth Press.
4. Erickson, C. K. (2007). *The science of addiction: From neurobiology to treatment.* New York, NY: Norton.
5. Kuhn, C., Swartzwelder, S., & Wilson, W. (2008). *Buzzed.* New York, NY: Norton.
6. McNeece, C. A., & DiNitto, D. M. (Eds.) (2005). *Chemical dependency: A systems approach* (3rd ed.). Boston, MA: Pearson.

The following group is related to addiction counseling, co-occurring disorders, and psychotherapy.

1. Beck, A. T., Wright, F. D., Newman, C. F., & Liese, B. S. (1993). *Cognitive therapy of substance abuse.* New York, NY: Guilford Press.
2. Bertolino, B., & O'Hanlon, B. (2002). *Collaborative, competency-based counseling and psychotherapy.* Boston, MA: Allyn and Bacon.
3. De Jong, P., & Berg, I. K. (2007). *Interviewing for solutions* (3rd ed.). Pacific Grove, CA: Brooks-Cole.

4. Ekleberry, S. E. (2009). *Integrated treatment for co-occurring disorders: Personality disorders and addiction.* New York, NY: Routledge.
5. Flores, P. (2008). *Group psychotherapy with addicted populations: An integration of twelve-step and psychodynamic theory* (3rd. ed.). New York, NY: Taylor and Frances.
6. Miller, W. M., & Rollnick, S. (2002). *Motivational interviewing* (2nd ed.). New York, NY: Guilford Press.
7. Nace, E. P., & Tinsley, J. A. (2007). *Patients with substance abuse problems: Effective identification, diagnosis and treatment.* New York, NY: Norton.
8. O' Hanlon, B. (2003). *A guide to inclusive therapy: Methods of respectful resistance dissolving therapy.* New York, NY: Norton.
9. Ryglewicz, H., & Pepper, B. (1996). *Lives at risk: Understanding and treating young people with dual disorders.* New York, NY: Free Press.
10. Todd, T. C., & Selekman, M. D. (Eds.). (1991). *Family therapy approaches with adolescent substance abusers.* Boston, MA: Allyn and Bacon.
11. Vaillant, G. C. (1995). *The natural history of alcoholism revisited.* Cambridge, MA: Harvard University Press.
12. Yalom, I. D., & Leszcz, M. (2005). *Theory and practice of group psychotherapy* (5th ed.). New York, NY: Basic Books.

There are both upsides and downsides to patients becoming knowledgeable about their diseases and therapy. On the positive side, educated patients may be able to express their symptoms to aid the clinicians. On the completely opposite side, clinicians have described in the scientific literature a syndrome called "Münchausen by Internet," where knowledge-savvy patients develop symptoms after searching the Internet literature.

References

Alcoholics Anonymous Big Book, Fourth Edition (2001). New York, NY: Alcoholics Anonymous World Services, Inc.

American Heritage Medical Dictionary (2007). New York, NY: Houghton Mifflin Harcourt.

American Psychiatric Association. *Diagnostic and statistical manual of mental disorders,* Fourth Edition, Text Revision (DSM-IV-TR) (2000). Washington, D.C., American Psychiatric Association.

Anthony, J. C., Warner, L. A., & Kessler, R. C. (1994). Comparative epidemiology of dependence on tobacco, alcohol, controlled substances, and inhalants: Basic findings from the national comorbidity survey. *Experimental & Clinical Psychopharmacology, 2,* 244–268.

Betty Ford Institute Consensus Panel (2007). What is recovery? A working definition from the Betty Ford Institute. *Journal of Substance Abuse Treatment, 33,* 221–228.

Brereton, A. (n.d.). Glossary of terms relating to autism and other pervasive developmental disorders. Retrieved November 28, 2010, from http://www.timeforafuture.com.au/fact_sheets/glossary.htm

Brick, J. & Erickson, C. K. (2009). Intoxication is not alwalys visible: An unrecognized prevention challenge. *Alcoholism Clinical and Experimental Research, 33,* 1489–1507.

Degenhardt, L., Coffey, C., Carlin, J. B., Moran, P., & Patton, G. C. (2007). Who are the new amphetamine users? A 10-year prospective study of young Australians. Addiction, 102, 1269–79.

Erickson, C. K. (2007). *The science of addiction: From neurobiology to treatment.* New York, NY: W. W. Norton & Company.

Grant, B. F. & Dawson, D. A. (1997). Age at onset of alcohol use and its association with DSM-IV alcohol abuse and dependence: Results from the National Longitudinal Alcohol Epidemiologic Survey. *Journal of Substance Abuse, 9,* 103–110.

Greenfield, S. F., Back, S. E., Lawson, K. & Brady, K. T. (2010). Substance abuse in women. *Psychiatric Clinics of North America, 33,* 339–355.

Harvard Mental Health Letter (January 2010). *Addiction in women.* 26(7).

HelpGuide.org. (n.d.). Drug abuse and addiction: Signs, symptoms, and help for drug problems and substance abuse. Retrieved October 9, 2010, from http://www.helpguide.org/mental/drug_substance_abuse_addiction_signs_effects_treatment.htm

HomeOffice.gov.uk. (n.d.). Class a, b, and c drugs. Retrieved November 28, 2010, from http://webarchive.nationalarchives.gov.uk/+/http://www.homeoffice.gov.uk/drugs/drugs-law/Class-a-b-c/

Koob, G. F. & Volkow, N. D. (2010). Neurocircuitry of addiction. *Neuropsychopharmacology Reviews, 35,* 217–238.

Kuhn, C., Swartzwelder, S., & Wilson, W. (2008). *Buzzed: The straight facts about the most used and abused drugs from alcohol to ecstasy* (Third Edition). New York, NY, W.W. Norton & Company.

Langston, J. W. & Irwin, I. (1986). MPTP: Current concepts and controversies. *Clinical Neuropharmacology, 9,* 485–507.

National Alliance on Mental Illness (2010). Dual diagnosis and integrated treatment of mental illness and substance abuse disorder. Retrieved November 28, 2010, from http://www.nami.org/Template.cfm?Section=By_Illness&Template=/TaggedPage/TaggedPageDisplay. cfm&TPLID=54&ContentID=23049

National Coalition for the Homeless (July 2009). Substance abuse and homelessness. Retrieved November 28, 2010, from www.nationalhomeless.org/factsheets/addiction.pdf

National Institute on Drug Abuse (n.d.). Club drugs. Retrieved November 28, 2010, from http://www.nida.nih.gov/DrugPages/Clubdrugs.html

SAMHSA (Substance Abuse and Mental Health Services Administration) (n.d.). Co-occurring disorder-related quick facts: Nicotine. Retrieved November 28, 2010, from coce.samhsa.gov/cod_resources/PDF/NicotineQuickFacts.pdf

SAMHSA (Substance Abuse and Mental Health Services Administration) (2009). Results from the 2008 national survey on drug use and health: National findings. Retrieved from http://www.whitehousedrugpolicy.gov/drugfact/cocaine

Shultes, R. E. & Hofmann, A. (1979). *Plants of the Gods: Origins of hallucinogenic use.* New York, NY: McGraw-Hill.

Sullivan, H. S. (1953). *The interpersonal theory of psychiatry.* New York, NY, W.W. Norton & Company.

Tuckman, B. (1965). Developmental sequence in small groups. *Psychological Bulletin, 63*, 384–399.

Tull, M. (2008). PTSD. The connection between PTSD and alcohol and drug use. Retrieved November 28, 2010, from http://ptsd.about.com/od/relatedconditions/a/drugalcohol.htm

World Health Organization. *The ICD-10 classification of mental and behavioural disorders: Clinical descriptions and diagnostic guidelines* (1992). Geneva, Switzerland: World Health Organization.

Yalom, I. D., *The theory and practice of group psychotherapy*, Fifth Edition (2005). New York, NY: Basic Books.

Index

hypervigilance, 84
hypomania, 18

MIP. *see* minor in possession (MIP)
MISA. *see* mentally ill substance abuser
   (MISA)
misperceptions, defined, 21
Misuse of Drugs Act (1971), 38
moderate drinking, defined, 26
mood stabilizers, 46
moral defects, 4
morphine, 35, 45, 47, 48
"Mother's Little Helper" (Rolling Stones),
   49–50
motivational enhancement therapy
   (MET), 97
motivational interviewing (MI), 15, 97,
   115–19, 130–31, 140–41
   see also change
mutual help groups. *see* fellowship
   groups

NA. *see* Narcotics Anonymous (NA)
Nar-Anon, 157–58
Narcan (naloxone), 47, 49, 100
narcissism, 17, 78
   see also narcissistic personality
   disorder (NPD)
narcissistic personality disorder (NPD),
   15, 90, 93–94
   see also antisocial personality disorder
   (APD)
Narcotics Anonymous (NA), 145, 159
National Institute on Alcohol Abuse and
   Alcoholism (NIAAA), 30
National Institute on Drug Abuse
   (NIDA), 39, 43, 57, 59
National Institutes of Health (NIH), 30,
   69
National Survey on Drug Use and Health
   (2005), 35
neuroadaptation, 1, 8, 9
neurobiology, 1, 30, 163
   see also frontal lobes; mesolimbic
   dopamine system (MDS)
neurochemistry, 4, 5–6, 9–10, 164
neuroleptics, 35
NIAAA. *see* National Institute on Alcohol
   Abuse and Alcoholism (NIAAA)
nicotine replacement therapy (NRT), 57,
   104–6
nicotine use and dependence
   adolescents and, 56–57, 70, 85
   alcohol use and, 35
   anxiety and, 81
   clinical depression and, 77
   cocaine and, 35

comorbidity and, 15, 86–87, 89
cultural differences about tobacco and,
   73
gateway drug theory and, 55–56
gender differences in tobacco use, 70
genetics and, 6
health effects of tobacco and, 70, 86
heroin use and dependence and, 45
"Joe Kool" advertisements, 54
medications to treat, 102–6
posttraumatic stress disorder (PTSD)
   and, 85
relapses and, 87, 164
schizophrenia and, 19, 83
signs of, 65
smoking cessation, 57, 104
vulnerability statistics, 70, 77, 86, 87,
   102
withdrawal from, 81
NIDA. *see* National Institute on Drug
   Abuse (NIDA)
NIH. *see* National Institutes of Health
   (NIH)
NIH Revitalization Act (1993), 69
nitrites, 60, 67
nitrous oxide, 60
nondrug addictions, 5
NPD. *see* narcissistic personality disorder
   (NPD)
NRT. *see* nicotine replacement therapy
   (NRT)
Nyquil (doxylamine), 46, 60–61

obsessive-compulsive personality
   disorder (OCD), 15, 19, 90
obvious intoxication, defined, 26
OCD. *see* obsessive-compulsive
   personality disorder (OCD)
opioid use and dependence
   adolescents and, 58
   antisocial personality disorder (APD)
   and, 92
   comorbidity and, 15
   medications to treat, 99–100
   morphine, 45
   overview of, 46–49
   posttraumatic stress disorder (PTSD)
   and, 84
   schizophrenia and, 83
   signs of, 66
   suicide and, 80
   withdrawal from, 48–49, 98–99
   see also specific drug; withdrawal
OTC. *see* over-the-counter (OTC) drugs